CHRISTINE ROBINSON MA PhD has taught Scots ... Edinburgh for many years. She also lectures ... University of the Highlands and Islands Millennium ...... is Director of Scottish Language Dictionaries (SLD). SLD is the organisation dedicated to the lexicography of Scots and Scottish English with stewardship of the *Scottish National Dictionary, A Dictionary of the Older Scottish Tongue* and the online *Dictionary of the Scots Language* www.dsl.ac.uk. In addition to lexicographical work, SLD has a lively outreach programme, supporting Scots in the community and in education.

Brought up in Perth, of Kincardineshire parents, and now living in West Lothian, she has first hand knowledge of a range of Scots dialects and has carried out a number of dialect research projects. She also has an interest in Older Scots. She is a committee member of the Scots Language Society, a Trustee of The Scots Language Centre, Chair of the Association for Scottish Literary Studies Language Committee, a member of the Literature Forum and a regular attendee at the Parliamentary Cross Party Group on Scots.

CAROL ANN CRAWFORD worked as an actor for many years before training as a Voice & Dialect Coach at The Central School of Speech & Drama, London. She has taught in many of the major drama schools as well as working in theatre in the UK and film in New Zealand.

She originally conceived the idea of a library of recordings of regional Scots for actors to consult. The Scots Language Resource Centre suggested she team up with Dr Chris Robinson and *Scotspeak* is the result of their collaboration.

The Scots Language Centre collects and distributes information about Scots; promotes Scots culture and encourages the use of spoken Scots through its web site and presence on a range of online platforms. Find out more at www.scotslanguage.com.

The recordings to accompany the text are available at
www.scotspeak.co.uk.

Scots Language Centre

Discover the world of Scots song and watch Scots films
Hear about the latest book and album releases
Find out about Scots dialects and Scots place names
Discover where to learn, hear and speak Scots
Explore social networking in Scots
Keep up to date with the latest news and events from the Scots language world

www.scotslanguage.com

Scottish Language Dictionaries research Scots texts from all periods of history, and record and analyse the language as it is spoken and written throughout Scotland today.

From this research we compile and maintain authoritative dictionaries of Scots, including the great historical dictionaries, *A Dictionary of the Older Scottish Tongue* and the *Scottish National Dictionary*, the scholarly single volume *Concise Scots Dictionary* and the handy *Essential Scots Dictionary*.

We maintain an active outreach programme and enquiries about the Scots Language are always welcome.

Our *Scuilwab* is specially designed for teachers, young people from nursery to university, and Scots language learners.

The nation's resource for the Scots language

www.scotsdictionaries.org.uk
www.dsl.ac.uk
www.scuilwab.org.uk

Scotspeak

A guide to the pronunciation
of modern urban Scots

> **GLASGOW**

> **EDINBURGH**

> **DUNDEE**

> **ABERDEEN**

Christine Robinson &
Carol Ann Crawford

Luath Press Limited
EDINBURGH
www.luath.co.uk

First Published 2001 by Scots Language Resource Centre
This edition 2011

ISBN 978 1 906307 30 1

The Publisher acknowledges subsidy from

Scottish
Arts Council

towards the publication of this book.

Published in association with

Scots Language Centre

Christine Robinson and Carol Ann Crawford have asserted their rights to be
identified as authors of this work in accordance with the Copyright, Design
and Patents Act, 1988.

Printed and bound by
Bell & Bain Ltd., Glasgow

Typeset in 11 point Times New Roman PS
by 3btype.com

Designed by Tom Bee

British Library Cataloguing-in-Publication Data.
A catalogue record for this book is available from the British Library.

ACKNOWLEDGEMENTS

Our greatest debt is to our informants. We cannot thank them enough for their patience and generosity. We are very grateful to the Scottish Arts Council and to the Gannochy Trust whose generosity enabled this Scots Language Resource Centre project to be carried out. Many thanks are due to Dr Caroline Macafee for her constructive criticism, advice and encouragement. Thanks also to Bobby More for the opening music (from *The Crimson Crown*) and to Christine Kydd for introducing each section with a song; to Dave Gray of the Sound Café for editing and technical wizardry; to Dr James M Scobbie at the Department of Speech and Language Sciences at Queen Margaret University College (ESRC funded: Scottish Vowel Length Rule Project R000237135) for help on intonation; the staff and students of Queen Margaret's Drama Department; and the students of the *Lothians Equal Access Programme for Schools* Summer School. In particular, the comments and suggestion made by Sine Robertson during the preparation of the first edition were invaluable.

CONTENTS

INTRODUCTION

We hope this project will be of interest to everyone who is fascinated by the richness and variety of spoken Scots. However, our original aim was to offer guidance to actors working on Scottish accents and this has affected how we selected and arranged the material.

Firstly we have opted to start by describing the major cities: Glasgow, Edinburgh, Dundee and Aberdeen. Our rationale is that contemporary drama often has an urban setting. So we begin with the accents most in demand. Dialectologists have tended to concentrate on rural accents, but city accents are important because of the number of speakers and because they act as core points from which change spreads into the surrounding areas.

Our focus is on accent, ie pronunciation. A study of dialect would also include a full description of differences in vocabulary and grammar. The recordings contain many dialect words (*weans, loon, strag, lumper,* etc) and examples of Scots grammar (*Ye never had nae claes*); we comment on these briefly but we have assumed that the writer will incorporate them into a character's speech as appropriate. Therefore, we concentrate on a description of sounds.

Secondly, we have tried to ensure that the recordings are not only authentic but also accessible. In other words, we have broken with the usual tradition in recording accents and dialects in that we did not seek out the strongest examples but selected more mainstream speakers who still exhibit the most typical features of each area. Where possible, we have tried to select male and female speakers with a range of age and voice qualities.

Thirdly, it was necessary to restrict the amount of detail to make it digestible. Within Edinburgh, for example, Leith, Morningside and the City Centre would claim to have distinctive accents. To give a comprehensive study of each city is beyond the scope of this project. It would have produced an inordinate amount of recorded material and would have reduced the usefulness of the book as a practical manual.

We have included some background information as well as a discussion of Scottish Standard English (SSE) and General Scots.

As a general rule, the use of Scots declines and the use of Standard English increases the higher up the social scale the speaker is or the more formal the occasion. We strongly recommend you look at the sections on Scottish Standard English and General Scots before you embark on a specific accent. The different areas have more in common than you might expect. Because one tends to highlight differences when one looks at dialects, these similarities are often overlooked. To avoid repetition, we have described widespread, recurrent features under SSE and General Scots. To ensure consistency and to simplify our descriptions, we have used the International Phonetic Alphabet. In case you are not already familiar with it, an explanatory chapter and an easy-to-follow key are provided.

Finally, we would like to say a heartfelt thank you to all our contributors, who not only gave up their time but also allowed us a privileged glimpse into their lives. Listening to the recordings, one is struck by the humour and resilience of the speakers. We hope you enjoy their conversation as much as we did.

THE ORIGINS OF SCOTS

Scots is descended from the Germanic language spoken by the Angles, Saxons and Jutes who invaded England in the fifth century CE. The Angles, with their Anglian dialect of Old English, pushed northwards to found the kingdoms of Mercia and Northumbria. From Northumbria, Anglian settlers moved on into south east Scotland during the seventh century.

By the ninth century, the language situation in Scotland was complex:

a)   In the far north, the Northern Isles and the Outer Hebrides, the Norwegian Vikings were in control.

b)   The Picts in the north east spoke a Celtic language probably related to Gaulish.

c)   The Scots, who spoke Gaelic, had, since the fifth century, been extending the kingdom of Dalriada from Ireland into Argyll and the Inner Hebrides.

d)   Strathclyde and the Central Lowlands were inhabited by Britons who spoke a form of Cumbric or early Welsh.

e)   In the Lothians and the Borders, the Northumbrian dialect of Old English was spoken.

Kenneth Macalpin, a Gaelic speaking Scot, united Scots and Picts in a single kingdom in 843 and Pictish and Cumbric began to wane. By 1034, in King Duncan's time, Scotland had predominantly Gaelic speakers north of the Forth and in the south west, Norse in the far north and Old English (Northumbrian dialect) in the Lothians and the Borders.

This Northumbrian Old English had been further differentiated from the dialects in the south of England by the incursions of the Danish Vikings. The Old Scandinavian group of languages was also part of the Germanic family; so it was likely that the Danish settlers in Yorkshire and the north-east of England could converse quite easily with the Old English population, in the way that Spanish and Italian speakers can understand each other today. Given the long and intimate contact between Old Danish and Northumbrian Old English, it is not surprising that the effects on Northumbrian were profound. Some of these even found their way into modern Standard English (the pronouns *they, their, them* and borrowed words like *law, root, skin, take, husband*) and the extent of Scandinavian influence on Scots, as a direct descendant of Northumbrian, is much more marked.

Old Scandinavian is heard in Modern Scots in a number of ways. The vocabulary includes many loans like *reek* (smoke), *tine* (lose), *ettle* (think, intend), *gate* (road). Sometimes a Scandinavian word was similar to an Old English word and reinforced the Old English word so that it remained in the north when it has been lost elsewhere: eg *bairn*. It is due to Scandinavian influence that so many /k/ forms survive in Scots where English has /tʃ/. So we get *kirk, birk*, as opposed to English *church, birch*. Even the Scots use of the preposition *till* (to) comes from Scandinavian influence.

Until the twelfth century, Gaelic was becoming increasingly dominant but, from the time of Malcolm Canmore (1057–93) and his English Queen, Margaret, *Inglis* began to supplant Gaelic as the language of the court and of government. Following the Norman Conquest, a large number of Normans, including the Bruces, the Balliols and the Comyns, were granted lands in Scotland. With the introduction of the feudal system and the establishment of burghs under David I, people of many languages were brought together to trade in safe commercial centres. Gaels, Scandinavians, Flemish weavers, Dutch craftsmen, Normans and Angles came together and gradually *Inglis* became the common tongue used by these different ethnic groups. Dutch and French words further increased and differentiated the vocabulary of this northern variety of *Inglis*.

By the second half of the fourteenth century, this was the dominant language spoken by all ranks of society outside the Highlands. It was spoken by the king and his court and it was used in official documents from 1398 onwards. Barbour's *Brus* (1376) marked the dawn of literary Scots and, within a century, Scots had overtaken Latin as the medium of literature and administration. By contrast, the north of England was looking to London for its cultural lead and the literary use of the northern dialect declined. Scotland, on the other hand, had an increasingly lively literary scene where the northern dialect flourished and continued to develop and grow, augmented by literary loans from Latin and French, until, in the sixteenth century, the Scots language had reached a peak in cultural achievement and status and the term *Scottis*, which had

THE ORIGINS OF SCOTS

until this time been used to refer to Gaelic, began to be used along-side *Inglis* to refer to the Lowland tongue.

But, from then on, it was all downhill for *Scottis*. First, God started to speak English! With the reformation came the widespread use of the Geneva Bible, in English. Then, the Union of the Crowns took the king and his courtiers south. Finally, with the Union of the Parliaments in 1707, the government moved south and all people of importance and power were perceived as English speaking. Influential Scots like David Hume went to great lengths to purge all trace of Scotticisms from their writing. Scots ceased to be a standard language and was seen as a mere collection of spoken dialects, the preserve of provincials and lower class persons. Speaking properly meant speaking English, even if the pronunciation remained distinctively Scottish.

Allan Ramsay, Robert Fergusson and Robert Burns kept the flame alive throughout the eighteenth century. In the nineteenth century, Scott, Hogg, Galt and the rather unfairly maligned 'kailyard'[1] school, who wrote chiefly on domestic and rural topics, took up the torch along with writers like Janet Hamilton, whose work is only now beginning to receive the acclaim it merits.

The twentieth century brought the birth of the Lallans movement and the Scottish Renaissance in which Hugh MacDiarmid was a towering figure. Lallans refers to the language of Lowland Scotland. MacDiarmid and others sought to enrich everyday language by using local words beyond their original areas and reviving older words which had dropped out of use. In a different but no less influential way, the Glasgow demotic poets, too, like Tom Leonard and Stephen Mulrine, have gone a long way in raising awareness of the language, its status and its possibilities. As a result, Scots has regained the confidence of poets as a suitable language for serious subjects.

Prose is having more of a struggle. For everyday writing, Scots have become accustomed to English. They have little in the way of models of Scottish prose writing to follow. Novelists like Sir Walter Scott left snatches of Scottish prose but it is all dialogue, nearly always in the mouth of characters of the lower social orders and embedded in an English narrative. So modern novelists like James Kelman, Matthew Fitt and Irvine Welsh are pushing back frontiers with their use of the vernacular.

---

[1] cabbage patch

A growing number of writers are making the transition from page to stage and screen – a natural progression, given their use of monologue and dialogue. Again, they are largely breaking new ground. Although we have Lyndsay's *Satire of the Three Estates* from the sixteenth century, Presbyterianism did not encourage theatre to develop in Scotland as it did in England. Nevertheless, we have modern classics such as Sidney Goodsir Smith's *The Wallace, The Bruce* by RS Silver and, more recently, the Scots version of *Cyrano de Bergerac* by Edwin Morgan, *Bondagers* by Sue Glover and works by Robert McLellan. A new generation of younger playwrights and screenwriters are emerging, all confidently employing With the high profile of such actors as Ewan McGregor and Robert Carlyle, there is less suspicion of Scots speech outside Scotland.

Much work has been done, and continues to be done, with a view to raising Scots once more to the status of a national language, to rationalise its spelling, to extend its vocabulary into every area of discourse, to have it taught in schools and used by the media. Yet, the sad truth is that in Scotland, the events of the last 400 years have left parents telling their children 'if folk are to get on the world nowadays, away from the ploughshafts and out of the pleiter,[2] they must use the English, orra[3] though it be' (*Sunset Song,* Lewis Grassic Gibbon).

However, there have recently been positive developments with regards to the Scots language. In 1996 a movement was started to have Scots recognised in the census as a language in its own right. Although the movement was unsuccessful in gaining a question on the 2001 census form, it proved that Scots was still very much a living language and that many people were willing to fight for it to be recognised. This led to The Scots Language Parliamentary Cross Party Group being formed with the intention of promoting the culture and heritage of the language. The ongoing campaign was successful and the 2011 census asked whether respondents could understand, read, write and speak Scots.

The Scottish and UK governments have made a commitment to support Scots under the terms of the European Charter for Regional or Minority Languages.

---

[2]   mire

[3]   strange, nondescript

DESCRIBING SPEECH

Language is, first and foremost, spoken. Writing is an attempt to represent the spoken word on a page, but spelling has not kept pace with changes in the spoken language. As a result, our spelling system is too confusing to be much use for describing sounds. Some of the letters in the normal alphabet can be used for more than one sound like the letter <c> in *circus, school, science*. Some sounds can be spelt in more than one way as in *kick, Rikki, cat* or *tie, spy, time, tight*. Some sounds have no letter to represent them and then pairs of letters have to be invented like <sh> as in *sheep* or <ch> which does service for two sounds as in *chip* and *loch* (and what about *Christmas* or *chiropodist*?). How many people realise that <th> has two pronunciations as in *thy* and *thigh*? To complicate things further, we have 'silent' letters in *knee, gnash, comb* and strange irregularities like *bough* and *cough*. We have chosen to use the International Phonetic Alphabet (IPA), so that we can be completely unambiguous. Most of the symbols are obvious and we provide examples of words as we go along to ease you into it gradually. Because it is used internationally, one or two of the symbols relate to other languages better than they do to Scots or English. For example, the sound that we usually spell with a <y> as in *yes, yet, yellow* (but not in *spy*) is represented by /j/. There are very few of these awkward ones though. The important thing to remember is to **forget spelling** and **listen** to what you and our informants actually say.

Where the International Phonetic Alphabet is used, slanting brackets / / indicate broad, generalised transcriptions of those sounds which are used to distinguish one word from another. Square brackets [ ] are used for closer, more exact representations of these sounds as they are actually used in speech.

Spellings are shown either by < > brackets or in italics.

In transcriptions of the recordings, square brackets around words or dots [...] denote a section which is inaudible or which we cannot transcribe with confidence. Sounds which are very lightly articulated or not articulated are shown in round brackets ( ) where this makes the transcription easier to follow. We also use round brackets for background noises, explanatory notes etc. The spelling of the transcriptions does not follow any strict spelling system as we wanted to make it easy to read while, at the same time, giving some flavour of the pronunciation. The unavoidable arbitrariness of spellings in transcriptions underlines the importance of the phonetic alphabet as a tool in describing accents.

Speech Sounds

Speech is composed of **consonants** and **vowels**. This section explains how we articulate or physically produce these sounds. It also contains definitions of the terms we use in our descriptions of the various accents.

Consonants

Consonants are easy to describe because they involve some kind of obstruction. Make a /p/ sound; and now a /b/. You will notice that you close your lips completely and this acts as a barrier to the breath before the /p/ or /b/ is released with a kind of mini-explosion. Therefore, these are known as **plosive** consonants or **stops**. Now try /s/ and /z/; the tongue is close to the roof of the mouth so that the channel for the breath is restricted and you hear friction. Therefore, these are known as **fricatives**. In sounds like /w/, the obstruction is not enough to make friction and the breath can flow more freely. These sounds are known as **approximants**. So in describing consonants, we look at the **manner** of making the obstruction.

Obviously, /p/ and /s/ are made in different parts of the mouth. So the **place** of articulation is important.

Then, as we have heard, /s/ and /z/ are both fricatives. They are both made in the same place, just behind the teeth. What is the difference between them? The answer is **voicing**. In other words, /s/ is made with the breath only, but for /z/ the vocal cords vibrate. Of course, in rapid speech this is not always easy to discern and there will be changes depending on the surrounding sounds.

When defining consonants we look at **voicing**, **place** and **manner**.

Voicing

Is the sound made with breath only or breath + voice? In other words, is it voiceless or voiced? You can **feel** this by putting your fingers on the front of your throat and making a /s/ then /z/. Can you feel the difference? What you feel with /z/ is vibration from the vocal cords. You can **hear** the difference by saying /s/ and /z/ with your hands over your ears. Sometimes, the voice gets switched off early and this **devoicing** means that a /z/ ends up a bit like a /s/. In the recordings final /d/ is often **devoiced** so that *retired* emerges as *retiret* (Joyce, Aberdeen) and *covered* as *covert* (Karen, Glasgow).

Note how many of the consonants can be regarded as voiced/voiceless pairs, like /b/ and /p/ or /v/ and /f/. One pair that often gets overlooked is the pair which share the spelling <th>. The initial sound is all that distinguishes between *thy* and *thigh*. *Thy* has a voiced sound /ð/ and *thigh* has the voiceless sound represented by the symbol **t**heta /θ/.

The voiceless consonants are /p/, /t/, /k/, /f/, /θ/ as in **thigh**, /s/, /ʃ/ as in **sh**e, /x/ as in lo**ch**, /h/, /ʍ/ as in SSE **wh**y and /tʃ/ as in **ch**ew.

The voiced consonants are /b/, /d/, /g/, /v/, /ð/ as in **thy**, /z/, /ʒ/ as in *rouge*, /r/, /l/, /j/ as in *yes*, /dʒ/ as in *judge*, /w/, /m/, /n/ and /ŋ/ as in *sing*.

Place

Here we describe where the obstruction occurs and which articulators are involved.

a) **Bilabial:** Both lips /p/, /b/, /m/.

b) **Labio-dental:** Upper teeth and lower lip /f/, /v/.

c) **Dental:** Tongue and upper teeth /θ/ /*thigh*, /ð/ *thy*.

d) **Alveolar:** Tongue and alveolar ridge (gum ridge which you can feel behind your upper teeth before the palate arches upwards) /t/, /d/, /n/, /l/, /s/, /z/.

e) **Post-alveolar:** Tongue draws back behind alveolar ridge as in RP and many Scots pronunciations of /r/.

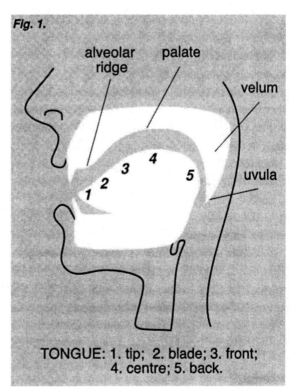

Fig. 1.

alveolar ridge   palate   velum   uvula

TONGUE: 1. tip; 2. blade; 3. front; 4. centre; 5. back.

f) **Palato-alveolar:** Tongue and back of alveolar ridge/front of hard palate /ʃ/ *show*, /ʒ/ *rouge*, /tʃ/ *chip*, /dʒ/ *jump*.

g) **Palatal:** Centre of tongue and hard palate /j/ *yes, yellow*.

h) **Velar:** Back of tongue and soft palate (velum) /k/, /g/, /ŋ/, /x/ *loch*. An important feature of all Scots accents except in the Highlands and Islands is the **dark /l/** given in detailed transcriptions as [ɫ]. As well as the alveolar articulation, the back of the tongue is raised towards the velum. This may be felt as a hollowing of the tongue. It gives a 'dark', swallowed quality to the sound. In RP you will hear a clear /l/ (purely alveolar) at the beginning of a word and a dark /l/ at the end. Contrast *lip* and *pill*. Most Scots use **dark /l/ in all positions**. This double articulation is also found in the **labiovelar consonants.**

i) **Labiovelar:** Lip rounding and the back of the tongue raised /w/ *witch*, /ʍ/ *which*.

j) **Glottal:** The glottis is the opening to the larynx or 'voice box'. It takes a lot of practice to feel what is going on so far back. When you say /h/ in isolation, you may be able to feel that it is glottal. If you are straining to lift something heavy you may make a **glottal stop**. When most of our speakers start an utterance with a vowel, there is a glottal stop [ʔ] before the vowel. The accents we look at frequently have a glottal stop as an alternative to /t/ in any position except the start of a stressed syllable.

If you are not sure where a sound is being articulated, say the sound and, without changing the position of the mouth, suck air in. You will feel cold where the articulators are closest together.

Manner

a) **Stops:** Two speech organs come together firmly, blocking the flow of air. Pressure builds up behind this closure so that an 'explosion' is heard when the organs part, hence the alternative name **plosives:** /p/, /t/, /k/, /b/, /d/, /g/. The nasal consonants are also stops but not plosives as the air escapes through the nose.

b) **Nasals** count as stops. If you say /m/, /n/ or /ŋ/ as in *sing* and hold your nose, you will feel a blockage, or stop, in the mouth. However, in nasals, the velum or soft palate is lowered to let air escape through the nose.

c) **Fricatives:** Friction is heard where two speech organs come close together, making a very narrow passage for the outgoing breath, /f/, /v/, /θ/ *thin*, /ð/ *then*, /s/, /z/, /ʃ/ *ship*, /ʒ/ *leisure*, /x/ *loch*, /h/, /ʍ/ *whale*.

d)   **Affricates:** These begin in the same way as a stop with firm contact between the two speech organs, but the release is gradual, creating friction /tʃ/ *church*, /dʒ/ *judge*.

e)   **Approximants:** These are made by 'approximating' two organs or bringing them closer together but not close enough to cause friction /l/, /w/, /j/ *yes* and RP /r/. This /r/ is also common in Scots speakers.

f)   **Laterals:** /l/ is also an approximant but it has one unique feature. Most sounds are made by the air flowing down the centre of the mouth. All the sounds of Scots and English have a **central** air-flow except the **lateral** consonant /l/ where the airflow is round the sides of the tongue. You can verify this by saying /l/ while sucking air inwards and feeling the sides of tongue grow cold.

/r/ needs to be thought about carefully. Often, when someone tries to imitate a Scots accent, they will emphasise the /r/ sounds by **rolling** or **trilling** them in an exaggerated fashion. This involves the tongue tip vibrating against the alveolar ridge. To native ears this sounds false. An alternative is the **tap** or **flap** which, as the name implies, involves a single tap of the tongue. This is often used between vowels. A better option is a **post-alveolar fricative** made with the tongue just behind the alveolar ridge, not actually touching, but close enough to produce friction or a **post-alveolar approximant** where the tongue tip curls just behind the alveolar ridge without touching it and without friction.

Vowels

Vowels are more difficult to describe because there is not the definite obstruction that you can feel in consonants. They are also subject to very fine, hard to hear variations and these subtle vowel differences are often very important from the point of view of regional variation. We have concentrated on the main features and have tried to keep the number of phonetic symbols to a minimum, but we suggest you pay particular attention to the vowels when working with the recordings.

Vowels are shaped by the lips and the tongue.

Lips

Are they **rounded, relaxed** or **spread?** Compare *who* and *he*. For *who* they will be tightly rounded, but for *he* they may be spread. Now try the phrase *Who would know aught of art?* and you'll feel your lips move gradually from the rounded position to neutral or relaxed. By whispering the vowels and missing out the consonants, you can enhance the sensation. Now try keeping your lips rounded or spread all the time – even when not appropriate – and notice how your voice alters because you are changing the shape of your mouth.

Tongue

The **vowel chart** is a way of trying to pinpoint the movements of the tongue. For the moment, forget about what your lips are doing and whisper *ha, hay, he*, keeping the tongue tip behind the lower teeth: you will feel the tongue rise up and forward.

With ha, the jaw is **lowered** and there is a big gap between the tongue and the roof of the mouth. This is an **open** or **low** vowel. With *he*, the jaw is **raised** and the tongue is much closer to the roof of the mouth. This is **close** or **high** vowel. *Hay* is between the two. Reverse the sequence and feel the tongue relax from **close** to to **open**. When we talk of **raising** we simply mean that the tongue is raised and **lowering** is simply the opposite. In the sentence *We eat lean meat*, these high vowels are comparatively more raised for a typical Glasgow accent contrasted with many other accents of Scots such as Dundee, where these vowels are comparatively lower.

Similarly, when describing a vowel as **front** or **back** we are referring to the highest point of the tongue. Try saying *oooo~eeee~oooo~eeee* and try to feel the backness and frontness. This positioning is what we mean when we describe *cat* as having a vowel which is more fronted in Glasgow and much further back in Aberdeen.

A vowel symbol which you will find very frequently in transcriptions is /ə/. This symbol is called *schwa* and it represents the indeterminate vowel that you find in unstressed syllables. It is not back, front, high or low but somewhere in the middle. If you have ever wondered whether a word was spelt *ible* or *-able*, what you really say is /əbl/.

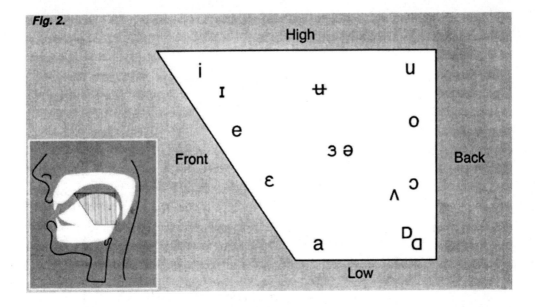

Fig. 2.

Many accents have a **posture** or **point of tension** which colours the voice. For example in north-east Scots, the jaw is often raised to give a close position (see above) with tension in the lip corners and the **placing** is typically back in the mouth. It might help you to picture an Aberdonian reluctant to open his mouth in the face of a North Sea wind.

Diphthongs

These involve the tongue moving from one vowel position to another. The three true diphthongs are found in *time, house* and *boy*. There is also a diphthong in *idea*, but Scots do not have so many occurrences of this diphthong as RP speakers, who have it whenever there is loss of /r/ in *fear* etc, because, for Scots speakers, the /r/ is not lost. However, many Scots do indeed put a schwa vowel in this position while retaining the /r/.

An interesting thing about SSE and Scots is the absence of any diphthong in *bait* and *boat*.

SCOTTISH STANDARD ENGLISH PRONUNCIATION

There are some features of pronunciation which are common to all Scots accents and others which are very widespread. Most Scots speakers move easily between their regional Scots and the pronunciations associated with Scottish Standard English (SSE). The more informal the situation, the higher the proportion of Scots forms. In a sense, they are bilingual. The same speaker might say *I told the children* or *A telt the weans*. This is known as **code-switching**. A more graduated response to changes in formality is described as **code-drifting**. We will start by looking at the features of SSE pronunciation and then describe regional features, taking SSE as our norm, rather than Southern Standard English with its associated accent, Received Pronunciation (RP).

SSE is the dialect which is typical of educated, middle class speech and is not particularly associated with any one region of Scotland. There is some regional variation in the accent of SSE speakers but the similarities are more important than the differences for present purposes. There is certainly a marked degree of uniformity in the speech of SSE speakers in Central Scotland. So middle class speakers in Glasgow and Edinburgh might sound very similar. SSE provides, moreover, a 'background' pronunciation: if you are not certain what the regional pronunciation of a word might be, a safe option is the SSE pronunciation, but keep the recommended regional mouth placing and intonation. This description is intended primarily for those who are not native speakers of SSE, but it may interest SSE speakers to take a closer look at what makes their accent distinctive.

Consonants

1. All Scots accents are **rhotic**. If there is an <r> in the spelling, there is an /r/ in the pronunciation. The most common pronunciation is the **post-alveolar approximant** or the **post-alveolar fricative** (see section on Describing Speech). Alternatively, it may involve a brief, light contact between the tongue and the alveolar ridge (just behind the upper teeth). This **tap** [ɾ] is heard at the start of words or between vowels. The strongly rolled /r/ which people often associate with a Scots accent is, in fact, fairly uncommon.

There is NO 'intrusive' /r/ as in *law(r) and order* [lɔ:rənd
ɔ:də]. Scots has the what-you-see-is-what-you-get [lɔ: ənd ɔ:rdər].
And if it is there, put it there [fe:r and skwe:r] *fair and square.*

Ex 1.   Phrases to practise: (answers at end of section)

I went to India and Burma after.

It is a far, far better car.

Her drawing was rather dirty.

2. A non-initial <ch> spelling sometimes represents /x/, which is
produced with the back of the tongue nearly, but not quite, touching
the soft palate as in *loch* /lɔx /. It is a voiceless velar fricative,
contrasting with the voiceless velar stop /k/ as in *lock* /lɔk/. With
the /k/ sound, actual contact is made. If you have difficulty, say
/k/, and then ease the tongue away, just a fraction or, if all else
fails, use /h/ instead.

Ex 2.   Phrases to practise: (answers at end of section)

It's dreich in Breich.

Is there a loch in Auchinblae or Ecclefechan?

Use your snochter-dichter.[1]

3. <wh> spellings represent /ʍ/. This can vary between a voiceless /w/, ie [ʍ] and [hw] in words like *when, where, which.* So
Scots distinguishes between *which* and *witch, whales* and *Wales,*
although this seems to be declining amongst younger speakers.

Ex 3.   Phrases to practise: (answers at end of section)

When and where do witches wear white?

Why do wise women whistle?

4. /l/ is usually dark. That is, the back of the tongue is raised as in
RP *dull.* SSE speakers usually have this kind of /l/ in all positions:

leap [ɫip], *peal* [piɫ].

Ex 4.   Phrases to practise:

Leonard lived long in Lilliesleaf.

Leaping lightly o'er the lea.

Look before you leap. Too late!

Len landed in Lochee.

5. In words containing <nch>, the /ntʃ/ is usually simplified to /nʃ/:

punch > punsh, branch > bransh, inch > insh etc.

Ex 5.   Phrases to practise:

I like to munch and crunch my French lunch.

Can you pinch more than an inch?

---

[1]   handkerchief

Vowels

1. The Scottish Vowel Length Rule

SSE does not usually distinguish between pairs of words like

pool ~ pull

caught ~ cot

psalm ~ Sam.

a)   The long, high, back, rounded vowel (RP *pool*) and its short equivalent (RP *pull*) are both short, high, rounded vowels in SSE and are usually fronted to /ʉ/.

b)   SSE has a short vowel in both *caught* and *cot* but the quality is usually closer to RP *caught* /ɔ/.

c)   In *Sam* and *psalm* words, again SSE has the short *Sam* vowel /a/, but slightly lower than many RP speakers would pronounce it.

SSE: /pʉl/   /kɔt/   /sam/

There are a few SSE speakers who have the *psalm ~ Sam* distinction but they do not always apply it to the same words as RP. For example *bath* and *grass* have a short front /a/ for these speakers. The safe option then, for non-Scots, is to avoid making this distinction in the accent of SSE.

(Of the few Scots who do have the *psalm, Sam* distinction, a very few have the *caught, cot* distinction and, of those who have both these distinctions, a very, very few distinguish between *pool* and *pull*.)

but

SSE speakers **do** make a distinction between pairs such as

brewed ~ brood

[brʉ:d] [brʉd]

Bruce ~ bruise, teeth ~ teethe, leaf ~ leave

[brʉs] [brʉ:z], [tiθ] [ti:ð], [ɫif] [ɫi:v]

car ~ cat, cart ~ cast

[ka:r] [kat], [ka:rt] [kast]

This is not as difficult as it appears since vowel length is predictable in SSE.

All vowels are short except

a)   when they are **word-final** (*sigh, brew,* etc). Once the length is thus defined as long, the vowels stay long even when you add inflectional endings like *-ed, -s.*

b)   **before voiced fricatives** /v/, /ð/, /z/, /ʒ/ as in *sleeve, breathe, rose, rouge.*

c) **before /r/.**

This is known as the **Scottish Vowel Length Rule** (SVLR).

The rule does not apply to the vowels /ɪ/, as in *living* and /ʌ/ as in *cur* but may apply to the vowel in *Kerr* etc, especially in stressed positions.

In practice, there may not always be full lengthening. We have not differentiated in our transcriptions between full and half-length but you may detect some inconsistencies even in a single speaker.

Ex 6. Which of the following words contain long vowels in SSE? (answers at end of section)

Tooth, breathe, believe, pass, sleeve, bruise, groove, pair, cry, Bruce, evil, anvil, burden, bear, barren, purr, pearl, good, food, sea, brewed, peace, peas, rude, rood, rued, brood, Susie.

(Do not be misled by spellings!)

2. Because the /r/ is always pronounced, Scots generally do not use the vowel /3:/ found where /r/ is lost in RP *bird, word, earth* [bɜ:d], [wɜ:d], [ɜ:θ]. Instead, they usually use either /ʌ/ (as in *but*) or /ɛ/ (as in *bed*) and always with the /r/. So, *bird > burd, word > wurd* BUT *earth > erth.*

[bʌrd]	[wʌrd]	[ɛrθ]
bird	word	earth

The spelling will help you to select the right one: <or>, <ur> and <ir> are [ʌr] as in *word, worth, curd, burn, bird, mirth.* Spellings with <er> (or <ear> where RP has [3:]) represent [ɛr] as in *herd, tern, Kerr, heard.* There are many examples in the recordings to help you. A few SSE speakers are beginning to use the /3/ vowel, but still with an /r/. Where used, this vowel may be subject to SVLR lengthening ([bɜ:rd], [wɜ:rd], [ɜ:rθ]). To many Scots these sound Anglicised or Americanised.

A few Scots distinguish between words with <ir> and words with <ur> or <or>. They have /ɪ/ as in *bit* in *bird* [bɪrd], *kirk* [kɪrk], *girl* [gɪrɫ] etc, contrasting with /ʌ/ in *word* [wʌrd], *burn* [bʌrn] etc. This is more common amongst older speakers and may be useful for period drama, but it is definitely declining in most areas.

Ex 7. Words to practise: (answers at end of section)

dirt, dirl, girl, gird, earn, birth, hurt, word, churn, turn, purl, worth, berth, heard, pearl, Perth.

3. Note that distinct vowels are preserved in *poor*, *pour* and *paw* with /pʉr/, /por/ and/pɔ/. Some words which you might expect to have /ɔ/ have /o/ in SSE: *pork*, *Ford*, *afford* but /fɔrk/.

Ex 8.   Words to try: (answers at end of section)
score, shore, flow, ensure, gnaw, floor, tour, tore, cure, torn, four, more, war, wore.

4. BAIT

The vowel in *bay*, *date* etc is usually realised as a monoph-thong [beː], [det], unlike RP which has a diphthong [beːɪ], [deːɪt].

5. BOAT

Similarly, the vowel in *know*, *boat* etc is realised as a mono-phthong [noː], [bot], unlike RP which has a diphthong [nəʊ], [bəʊt].

6. The unstressed vowels in SSE show a greater variety than in RP. Where RP would use /ə/ in *honest*, *hammer*, *between*, *Christmas*, SSE could have /ɔnɪst/ or /ɔnʌst/, /hamɪr/ or /hamʌr/, /bɪtwin/, /krɪsmas/, krɪsmɪs/ or /krɪsrmʌs/, although /ə/ would be a safe option, if you are unsure.

7. The unstressed final vowel, usually pronounced /ɪ/ in RP in words like *pretty, happy, falconry* and words with the suffix *-ly* etc usually end in /e/ for SSE speakers and may be raised after a preceding high vowel.

Diphthongs

Diphthongs obey the Scottish Vowel Length Rule.

1. TIME

The RP diphthong /aɪ/ as in *price* appears as /ʌi/ in SSE. When lengthened it is realised as [aːe]. So you get a contrast between *tide/tied* [tʌid]/[taːed]. What would happen with *side/sighed*?

2. HOUSE

RP /aʊ/ as in *mouth* becomes /ʌu/. It too may be lengthened in words like *cow, tower, rouse* but the vowel quality is unchanged.

3. BOY

RP /ɔɪ/ as in *choice* becomes /ɔe/. Again, the lengthened form in *boy, noise, Moir* keeps the same vowel sound as the short form *Boyd, choice, soil*.

Answers to exercises

Ex 1. [aːe wɛnt tə ɪndɪə ənd bʌrma aftər]

[ɪt ɪz a faːr faːr bɛtər kaːr]

[hʌr drɔːɪŋ wɔz raðər dʌrte]

Ex 2. [ɪts drɪx ɪn brɪx]

[ɪz ðer a lɔx ɪn ɔxənbɫe ɔr ɛkəɫfɛxən]

[jʉz jər snɔxtər dɪxtər]

Ex 3. [ʍɛn ənd ʍeːr dʉ wɪtʃəz weːr ʍʌit]

[ʍaːe dʉ waːez wɪmən ʍɪsəɫ]

Ex 6. breathe, believe, sleeve, bruise, groove, pair, cry, evil, bear, barren, pearl, sea, brewed, peas, rued, Susie.

Ex 7. [dʌrt dʌrɫ gʌrɫ gʌrd ɛrn bʌrθ hʌrt wʌrd tʃʌrn tʌrn pʌrɫ wʌrθ bɛrθ hɛrd pɛrɫ pɛrθ]

Ex 8. [skoːr ʃoːr ɫoː ənʃʉːr nɔː ɫoːr tʉːr toːr kjʉːr toːrn foːr moːr wɔːr woːr]

GENERAL FEATURES OF THE PRONUNCIATION OF SCOTS

In addition to the SSE features just described, the following features are common to many of the accents of Scots. You may like to start listening to the recordings as you read this section. Where the individual accents (Glasgow, Edinburgh, Dundee, Aberdeen) deviate from these general features, the differences will be identified in the detailed description of each accent.

Consonants

1. Except at the start of a stressed syllable, a glottal stop [ʔ] may be used instead of [t].

but [bʌʔ] *bucket* [bʌkəʔ] *patter* [paʔər] *glottal* [glɔʔət]. You will hear it in phrases like *going tae school*, where, although the /t/ is at the beginning of a word, it is not in a stressed position. In connected speech, it is essential to listen and try not to think about the written word.

2. In *-ing* words, final /ŋ/ is often replaced with /n/: *climbin, everythin, mornin*.

3. Loss of /l/, by a process known as l-vocalisation, is very common. It has happened in RP and SSE in words like *walk* and *talk*. Scots takes it a step further. In words such as wall, ball, where SSE would have /wɔl/ and /bɔl/, the /l/ disappears and the resulting Scots words are either /wɔ/, /bɔ/ etc, rhyming with SSE *saw*, (Glasgow, Edinburgh) or /wa/, /ba/ etc, rhyming with SSE *spa*, (Dundee, Aberdeen).

/l/-vocalisation also occurs in *folk > fowk* and there may be a change of vowel [fʌuk]. Similarly *golf > gowf, gold > gowd*.

4. /v/-deletion may occur as in *have > hae, give > gie, silver > siller*.

5. /nd/ may be simplified to /n/ in all positions: *and > an, candle > cannel/caunnel, round > roun /roon*.

6. /ld/ may be simplified to /l/ word finally, especially when the following word begins with a consonant: *cold > caul(d), old > aul(d)*.

7. Where words begin with the voiced <th-> /ð/, as in *the, that, this,* the /ð/ sound may be lost. This happens most often in pronouns and articles, especially after alveolar consonants /t/, /d/, /s/, /z/, /n/, /r/, /l/ at the end of the preceding word: *I telt (th)em; wha said (th)at?*

Vowels

MEET/BEAT, BIT, BAIT, BET, CAT

/i/, /ɪ/, /e/, /ɛ/, /a/ are generally similar to SSE although the exact pronunciation will depend on the mouth position characteristic of the particular region. Unfortunately, the words they are used in are not always the same:

a)   In some words with an <ea> spelling and an /ɛ/ pronunciation in SSE, the /ɛ/ is replaced with /i/ in *bread > breid, dead > deid* etc.

b)   SSE /o/ is often replaced with /e/ in *no > nae, so > sae, alone > alane, stone > stane, whole > hale, home > hame, ghost > ghaist, sore > sair* etc.

c)   SSE /ɔ/ often goes to /a/ where there is a following /p/, /b/, /m/, or /f/ as in *drap, Rab, Tam, aff, saft.*

d)   SSE /a/ may be replaced with /e/ in *father > faither, family > faimly, apple > aipple, yard > yaird, married > mairrit, part > pairt* etc.

e)   Sometimes final /e/ is replaced with /ʌi/ as in *pay > pey, stay > stey, way > wey*. This diphthong also appears in *baillie > bailie, jail > jile.*

Back Vowels

1. HOUSE/HOOSE

Where SSE has the /ʌu/ diphthong, *house*, Scots has the fronted /ʉ/, *hoose*. For many Scots, this is the same vowel as they use when they select an SSE form for *book, good* and *food.*

2. MOON/MUIN

Where SSE has /ʉ/ associated with an <oo> spelling, Scots may have a more fronted and unrounded pronunciation: *good> gid, moon>min*. This is usually associated with a <u> or <ui> spelling: *guid, muin*. In the north east area you even find *gweed* (good), *skweel* (school) etc. In the city, this is becoming rare although in both Dundee and Aberdeen we found *do>dee.*

3. COT, CAUGHT

The tendency to close the jaw in /ɔ/ words to give /o/ (*pork, ford*) noted in SSE vowels is generalised so that where SSE has /ɔ/ as in *cot, caught, cod, rod* many accents of Scots raise this vowel to /o/ so that *cot/caught/coat* sound the same, as do *cod/code, rod/road*. This feature seems to be most consistently developed in the Glasgow area although it does appear to some extent in all our speakers. Both forms may occur in the same speaker and/or the raising may sometimes be partial so that you may hear *cot* half-way between [kɔt] and [kot]. Some speakers may show raising in some words but not others.

4. GROW

Where SSE has /o/, often, but not always associated with an <ow> spelling, Scots may have a diphthong /ʌu/ as in SSE *how*: *grow, row, hoe*. (Do not confuse these with the words which have a diphthong in SSE and the /ʉ/ monophthong in Scots: SSE *how* > Scots *hoo*, SSE *cow* > Scots *coo*.)

5. PULL

In some of these words, 1-vocalisation may be found *pull* > *pu*, but, where 1-vocalisation does not take place, the SSE /ʉ/ before /l/ becomes /ʌ/ as in *bull, pull* etc, which in Scots rhyme with *dull*.

6. UMBURELLA [sic]

You will often hear an extra /ə/, particularly before /r/ and between /r/ and /n/, /m/ or /l/ as in *arm* [e:rəm], *corn* [ko:rən] *world* [wʌrət], but sporadically in other positions *film* [fɪɫəm].

Diphthongs

l. TIME

These words are similar to SSE

2. HOUSE

As explained above, HOUSE words have a monophthongal /ʉ/ but an /ʌu/ diphthong can be heard some SSE /o/ words such as *row, grow*.

3. BOY

Most of these words are the same as in SSE but there is an interesting group of words, many of French or Dutch origin, which join the TIME words. So *oil* sounds the same as *aisle*. Other examples include *boil, join* and *hoist* which become *bile, jine* and *hyst*.

4.

The tendency to slip in an extra little vowel, noted in 6. above, can produce a diphthong, or even an extra syllable, especially after /i/ or /e/ before /r/:*fear* [fiər], *rain* [reən].

GRAMMAR

We thought you might be more comfortable with any unfamiliar bits of Scots grammar if you were introduced to a few of the rules. It differs from English grammar in a number of ways. Many of the features which are looked down on are, in fact, highly pedigreed survivals from Old English. Sometimes the process of language change, operating in both Scots and English, may be more advanced in one language than the other, or may have affected different words. This accounts for most of the differences in past tenses and past participles. The following brief account explains just a few of the features of Scots grammar which can be heard in the recordings.

Negatives

To make a negative, our speakers nearly always add *-nae* (Glasgow, Edinburgh) or *-na* (Dundee, Aberdeen) where English speakers would use *-n't*:

> *He wisnae a fill-the-joug.* (Christie)
> *We didnae ken.* (Sean)
> *They dinna eat very often.* (Barbara)

Never is used in the sense of *not* with the past tense. So

> *The snake never came oot* (Barbara)

only refers to one particular occasion and may be translated as *The snake didn't come out*. There is no emphasis intended.

As in many regional varieties of English, double negatives are often used to emphasise negativity rather than cancelling each other out as in SSE.

> *Ye never had nae claes.* (Stanley)

Regional and SSE speakers usually prefer *It's no(t) my life.* (Maureen) to the English *It isn't my life*. Barbara has *It's nae gettin* rather than *It isna gettin*.

Number

You may find a noun in the singular where you would expect a plural. This is particularly common with measurements of distance or time preceded by a numeral or a word indicating number.

> *a couple year ago; a few year.* (Joyce)

Verbs

Past tenses

Where English uses -*ed* to form a part tense or past participle, Scots very often uses -*it*:

[I] aye workit in the fish trade. (Stanley)

As anyone who has ever learned a foreign language knows, strong verbs, the ones that change their vowels to make past tense or past participle, are very difficult to learn. English and Scots have both been making themselves easier over the years. Some strong verbs have become weak like Old English *smeocan* (to smoke). It used to have *hit smiecth* (it smokes), *hit smeac* (it smoked) *hie smucon* (they smoked) and the past participle was *smocen*. Thank goodness English is getting easier!

If we compare the Scots past tense and past participle of *gi(v)e*, which for many speakers are both *gied*, with the English *gave* and *given*, we can see that, in this instance, Scots is just a bit further down the road of simplification.

I gied him the ticket. (Nan)

What Nan is doing in

A never telt big John

is making a weak verb out of *tell*. Occasionally Scots lags behind. For example, many Scots still use *gotten* as the past participle of *get*.

There is a simplification process in operation when Charlie says:

You done well there

and

I've actually did a little sales myself.

He wants the past tense and the past participle to be the same – he just hasn't quite settled on which form to choose. And this is how language change often works. There may be a period of choice before one form becomes dominant. It is probably better to think of these anomalies as change in progress rather than bad grammar.

Auxiliary Verbs

In Edinburgh and the Borders, you will often hear combinations of auxiliary verbs which would not be acceptable elsewhere. These are well established features of the grammar of these regions:

We used to could see across the Newcastle sheds. (Jenny)

Narrative Present Tense

This is often used to bring vividness into a story. Note that the endings are not the same as in the ordinary present tense. The narrative present tense has an -s ending throughout:

We gets aff the train. (Nan)

A speaker can switch from past to narrative present in the same sentence:

My dad knew there was something wrong wi us, you know, an he's sayin to me . . . (Maureen)

Subject/verb agreement

Where the subject is a plural noun, *is* and *was* are commonly used. Oddly, *we was* is a regular alternative to *we were* but *is* is never used with *we*.

We was robbed!

Demonstratives

Thay (those) as a plural of *that* is another survival from Old English:

We were aa slim in thay days (Annie)

Thon (sg. and pl.) is an additional demonstrative, carrying a sense of being far distant from both speaker and hearer.

thon widden seats (Nan)

Pronouns

The unstressed first person plural possessive (our) is *oor*, *wir* or *wur*:

wir cakes (Jean)

The third person plural reflexive pronoun (themselves) is *thirsels*:

as they would call thirsels (Charlie)

The plural form *us* may replace *me*:

My dad knew there was something wrong wi us. (Maureen)

You will observe a number of other features of grammar and idiom in the recordings which might not come naturally to you if you are not a native Scots speaker. However, if you are working from a script, the writer will guide you.

GLASGOW

The accent described here is also found in Clydebank, Rutherglen, Paisley and Renfrew. Many of the features extend into Lanarkshire and Ayrshire. There is a marked degree of awareness of the social implications of using dialectal forms. Middle class speakers tend towards SSE and, for most speakers, the relative number of SSE forms will increase with the formality of the situation. Many speakers can code-switch instantaneously from strong dialect to SSE. Glasgow has probably suffered from accent stereotyping more than any other area of Scotland. In reality, there is a lot of variation within the city. Charlie is quite different from Nan and neither of them sounds like Rab C Nesbitt.

Intonation

The intonation pattern of Glasgow is very distinctive. There is a lot of variation in pitch. This is much more marked than in other accents. Stressed syllables 'occur as scoops down in pitch'[1] with a rise up again. This produces a rising pattern so that even declarative utterances or statements have a rising tune. For questions, therefore, the voice has to rise quite steeply to mark the exaggerated question rise from the normal rise:

Umbrella Bridge in Argyle Street? (Karen)

Charlie shows some fairly abrupt rises and drops which are like swoops rather than steps. Despite his careful articulation, he demonstrates quintessentially Glasgow intonation, with lots of scoops:

The whole office knew. (Charlie)

Often there will be a level section in the middle of a statement with a rise at the end:

and he was payin me... em like five hundred pouns a week.

For emphasis, Glasgow speakers stretch the vowels and increase the volume, often accompanied by the scoop and rise intonation: *an these weans were dead smiley* (Karen) where the [ɛːi] in *smiley* is subjected to the Glasgow drawl; *it's mostly sales* (Charlie) where the [eː] is lengthened or *he was telling me* (Charlie) with a long [ɛː]. These long vowels are independent of the Scots Vowel Length Rule.

---

[1] Brown, Currie and Kenworthy p19.

The Glasgow drawl, with its 'elastic vowels' and rising inflection prompts comment from Tom Leonard in his poem *Teatime*:

ahm thaht depehhhndint

hingoanti ma vowwwwulz

hingoanti ma maaaammi

The stretching of the vowels makes it easy to hear the glides down and up in pitch. A tip for non-natives is to think of the appropriate inflection for reciting a list:

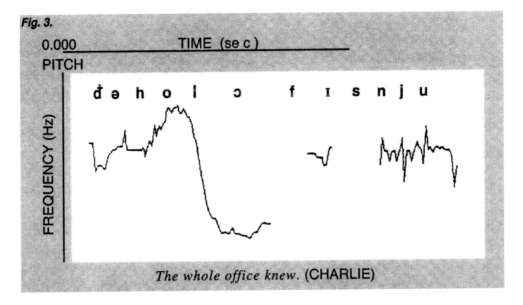

The whole office knew. (CHARLIE)

A pound of tea

A loaf of bread

A bottle of wine

A pound of butter

Now try these statements keeping the scoop down on the bold vowel and up on the last vowel in each of the words underlined:

Scotland's *famous* for its *scenery*.

Scots are *known* for their *hospitality*.

Mouth Position

The position of the tongue in the mouth is similar to that of SSE or, if anything, slightly forward. You may find it helps to think of the voice being 'focused' up and forward onto the alveolar ridge. In some speakers you may hear nasality.

So far as our speakers are concerned, the lips show some loss of rounding with the fronted vowel in BOOT /ʉ/ words, but the back vowels of BOAT /o/ words and COT, CAUGHT /ɔ/ words show quite clear rounding. There is minimal spreading for the high front MEET, BEAT /i/ vowel. The lips are fairly relaxed.

The lower jaw may be slightly protruded (Macafee 1983 p35), and this is consistent with the forward position of the tongue.

Consonants

1. The use of the **glottal stop** [ʔ] as a variant of /t/ is very frequent and even if alveolar contact is still audible, the /t/ may still be strongly glottalised. This is most commonly noticed between vowels: *pretty, gettin, water,* and at the end of words: *fat, cut, feet, went, permanent, polite,* but it can occur anywhere except at the start of a stressed syllable. So you get glottalisation in *Coatbridge, its.*

An incomplete articulation of /t/, where contact with the alveolar ridge is not enough to build up plosion, may produce a tap [ɾ] between vowels. So you get pronunciations like *burrur* [bʌɾʌɾ]. Overuse of this feature would produce a caricature of the accent.

2. Dental fricatives:

a) /θ/ is often pronounced as [h]: *thing > hing.*
The [h] can become the voiceless equivalent of the following consonant.

b) /ð/ may become a tap [ɾ] both initially and intervocalically *ra morra* (Nan), *bother > borrer* (Nan). If there is a neighbouring /r/ there may be assimilation: *brother > brorr, mother > morr.* There are further good examples of this from Nan.

c) TH-dropping results in loss of /θ/ in *Ro(th)esay, wi(th)* etc, and loss of /ð/ in *clothes > claes.*

3. After vowels or where it is a syllable in its own right, /l/ may be become more like [w] or even [o]: *little* [ɬɪʔw] or [ɬɪʔo].

4. There may be devoicing of /d/ at the end of words: *bastart.*

5. Features which appear to be on the increase are /x/ being replaced with [k], and /ʍ/ being replaced with [w]. So the distinction between pairs of words like *loch~lock* and *which~witch* is being eroded.

6. In some speakers, /s/ is formed with the blade or front, rather

than the tip, of the tongue, making it closer to /ʃ/. You can hear this in Nan's *A wis staunnin (th)ere*.

Vowels

There is lengthening of some vowels which the SVLR would predict as short:

smellin o fat [smɛtənə faːʔ] *post office* [post ɔːfɪs]

Vowel quality follows the generalisation of Scots vowels given above. In addition, the following features may be found in Glasgow speakers:

1. FAIR

The vowel which is most distinctively Glasgow in quality is the [ɛːr] where other Scots accents would have [eːr] so *that fair* [fɛːr] and *chair* [tʃɛːr] rhyme with *Kerr* [kɛːr] and *Kerr* and *care* sound the same.

2. WATER

/a/ is used after /w/ as in *squaad, waatter, waant, waash* where SSE would use /ɔ/.

3. Before /r/ and /n/, where SSE and eastern accents of Scots have [a(ː)] ~ [ɑ(ː)], Glasgow has [ɔ(ː)] as in *caur* (car). Nan has this in *staunnin* (standing). The same vowel is found in the Glasgow pronunciation of *tattie* (potato) and *hauf* (half). It is worth listening for other words which may join this category.

4. COT, CAUGHT

The words usually associated with the /ɔ/ sound may have [o(ː)]: *affoard, coarner, hoalidays, coaffin*, as mentioned under the general features of Scots.

5. Unstressed final /o/ in Glasgow appears as [ʌ] or [a]: *barra, fella, morra*.

6. CAT

Compared with Edinburgh, [a(ː)] as in *fat, back*, Glasgow is noticeably fronted.

Diphthongs

1. TIME

The SSE /ʌi/ as in *time, bite* is realised as [ɛi] and the first part of this is centralised. If there is lengthening, as in *buy, pie* it is lowered to [aːe]. This means there is less of a glide.

2. *Poison, oil, boil, spoil, join, hoist, joist* are all pronounced with the TIME diphthong.

3. BOY

The usual pronunciation for words with an <oi> or <oy> spelling, like *employ*, varies between [ɔe], as in SSE, and [oe].

4. HOUSE

Where the SSE /ʌu/ is not monophthongised to [ʉ] as in *hoose* it becomes fronted to [əʉ] or, increasingly in young speakers, even further.

Syllable boundaries

In some popular representations of Glasgow speech, such as Stanley Baxter's *Parliamo Glasgow* and Tom Leonard's poetry the Glasgow trait of running words together is parodied:

'sofficolraday' – Stanley Baxter, *Parliamo Glasgow*.

'dizny day gonabootlika hawf shut knife' – Tom Leonard, *The Miracle of the Burd and the Fishes*.

Our speakers show this, but not in any exaggerated way. They quite often detach a final consonant and make it the first consonant of the following word:

A didn't like it a-tall (Charlie).

The pronouns *I* and *my* are *A* and *ma*.

The negative ending in *dinnae, cannae* etc is [ne].

The vowel in <aw> words *braw, snow* and after loss of /l/ in *a(ll), ba(ll)* is [ɔ:].

The vowel of final *-ly* in *lovely* is [e] or [ɪ].

The final vowel in *barrow/barrae, window/windae* is [a] or [ʌ].

Of is reduced to [e].

GLASGOW RECORDINGS

Karen

Tae get through my last year at school, A worked in a chip shop... for a year... em... (laugh) which was... it was disgusting. Ye'd come home at night smellin o fat. An... an when A left... aw... they poured... ye know fish juice all down ma back an A went home absolutely mingin,[1] eggs stuck in ma head an things, so... it was lovely gettin on the bus ye know... the last bus home (laugh) an A'm [h]... absolutely mingin o fish. Oh... it was horrible, it was absolutely horrible. An they picked me up an threw me in wi all the the the chips that were cut for the next day, So A was drippin. Eh... absolutely soakin o water... the smell o the fish, A had eggs and Tunnock's Teacakes [on me]... Oh God, it was disgustin!

Em... an then A worked in shoe shops, an A worked in various shoe shops all through Glasgow em... an some in really deprived areas... em... A worked for one specific company eh called Feet & Co... Ye can tell by the name, eh? (laugh) Eh... an they had, like loads o branches all through Lanarkshire an Glasgow. Eh... An when A went tae college they took me on every summer, you know, so it was like ma wee summer job... em... an for a while A was in... Ma first summer there A had a permanent job in Coatbridge which was fine, you know, that was... that was OK. Eh... the next year they said they'd take me on for like, holiday cover, so em... A ended up underneath Umbrella Bridge in Argyle Street? A was in there an that was disgustin. It was really disgustin: ye'd walk out the door and there'd be tramps sleepin underneath yer trays o shoes... an ye know under there all the... the fumes... gather so ye'd blow yer nose an all this dirt would come out yer nose. The walls were all foosty[2] an... oh, it was horrible. Em... An ma first day workin there... em... a woman came in an she'd

---

[1]   stinking, disgusting

[2]   mouldy

*two wee bits o weans[3] an eh, you know, they'd they'd
stuffed, all their hair was cut off and they'd stuff [da]...
all dabbed on their heads an... em... oh, it was it was just
such a shame. They thought that this was normal. An their
mammy had like shite all up her jacket. It was all covered,
oh, it was just disgustin. It was really... it would have turned
yer stomach. An these weans were dead smiley an everythin,
ye know, an yer heart just went out tae them. Em... an
(th)en, about a day or two after that a guy walked in... an
he had, like, a big scar right down his face an eh... as he
walked in the door he shoved this thing up his sleeve.
So ma heart immediately went intae ma mouth, ye know.
A thought 'God, we're gonnae get done over.' An em... aw,
ma heart was poundin an he came up tae me an he says,
'Eh... eh... D'ye sell kids' clogs, hen?' An' A was like, 'Em...
no, A'm sorry we don't stock them in the... d'ye know
they're not in season this summer.' An' he was like, 'Right,
fine.' An as he walked out the door, he pulled out this
bottle o Buckfast... this was him tryin tae be polite, ye know.
An A thought A was gonnae get slashed, he was gonnae try
an rob the place, ye know, so ma heart was poundin. So...
eh... from there, they shiftit me up tae Sauchiehall Street
an A got pit intae the Savoy Centre, where ye had auld
grannies fightin over slippers... So when... ye'd walk into the
stock room and basically it was just like a wee box, ye know,
the whole thing it was... [t]... a tiny wee corner unit, ye
know, in in the Shoppin Centre and ye'd walk intae the
stock room an everything just fell on yer head cos it was so
crammed an aw God... So I was there for about a fortnight.
Eh... and then they moved me to Easterhouse an eh A was
there for the rest o the summer. An A couldn't believe it ye
know... eh... Within... whit, the first week an a half o bein
there, a guy had got slashed outside the shop... em... ye
know, fightin in the Shoppin Centre and he got slashed an
stuff. Ye had tae get the security guy... guard tae take ye tae
the Post Office which was basically two doors away. Ye had
to call [the] Security Guard tae take ye down with all this*

---

3   children

money an stuff so ye wouldn't get jumped... eh...
There was women comin in, A mean eh... some o them
are so deprived it's unbelievable... women comin in with
three an four kids an they've thought up schemes tae try
an, like, ye know, em steal a pair o seven pound shoes for
their kids to go back to school. An it... it... jist made me
realise how, ye know, how deprived and how poor some
people are. Eh... ma heart went out tae them rather than
[the] thought of... thinkin about punishin them, ye know.
Em... A [just] in some ways A thought, 'Well good on them
for for actually comin up with somethin that's so inventive,
ye know, (laughs) cos Am tellin ye the schemes were
unbelievable, ye know... em... But it was their way
of survivin.

Things to note in Karen's Glasgow
Intonation

Her intonation is typically Glasgow. The 'scoop and rise' shows up
clearly. A good unexaggerated example is the final phrase,

> *but it was their way of survivin.*

There is a good example of the use of scoop and vowel length in

> *he got slashed an stuff.*

Consonants

1. Karen frequently glottalises /t/ or completely substitutes a glottal
stop for /t/.

Glottalised /t/: *at school, permanent, dirt*

Complete substitution: *fat, absolutely, it, gettin, cut,
Coatbridge*

She also uses glottal stops where certain consonant clusters
arise across word boundaries, effectively making the second word
an unstressed part of the first, a simplification which is taken to
its extreme in *going to* > *gonnae* and is at an intermediate stage
in *tryin tae*, where the /t/ is more glottal than alveolar.

The /t/ is less likely to be replaced with [ʔ] where it marks a
past tense or past participle: *worked* [wʌrkt], *slashed* [slaʃt], but
some glottalling may occur in the Scots *-it* past tense/past participle: *shiftit*.

In *last year* and *last bus*, the consonant cluster is simplified so
that the /t/ is completely lost and no glottal is substituted. However,

where the /st/ is being shared across a syllable boundary, the /t/ is preserved: *disgustin, foosty.*

2. Notice also that there is a tendency to devoice a past tense /d/: *covered* [kʌvʌrt].

3. Karen shows some TH-dropping:

an these weans [aniːz wenz]

he walked in the door [hi wɔkt ɪnə doːr]

comin up wi somethin [kʌmɪnʌpwɪ sʌmm]

4. She shows a very slight tendency towards the Glasgow tap in *you can tell by the name* and *the last bus home.*

5. /l/ after a vowel or as a syllable in its own right shows a tendency to be realised as [o]: *horrible, unbelievable.* In *bottle o Buckfast* there is the velar darkening with the lip-rounding of /o/ but the alveolar contact is still audible.

6. Usually, Karen has the SSE [ʍ] but in *for a while* she has [w].

Vowels

1. Karen demonstrates the Glasgow drawl. Where the Scottish Vowel Length Rule predicts a long vowel, lengthening may be very marked. Notice particularly how vowels which you would expect to be short may also show some degree of lengthening on a rising intonation:

smellin o faːt; hoːliday cover; dead smiːley etc.

2. Note the extra vowel in *umbrella* [ʌmbərɛɬa].

3. Where the /v/ in *of* is lost you may hear [e] as in *the rest o the summer.*

4. CAT

Karen has quite a front [a] in *fat, back, Glasgow* etc.

5. BIT

In line with most Scots accents, Karen lowers /ɪ/ as in *fish, chips.*

Words to listen to

school, fat, mingin, fish, chips, Glasgow, feet, holiday, umbrella, dirt, weans, normal, mammy, smiley, done over, season, shiftit, grannies, Post Office.

Charlie

CHARLIE: *It's mostly sales A want. A... a... at the the end of the day it's... it's sales A want tae be out in the field, you know [that]... A don't think A could handle sittin in an office... from nine tae five for the rest of ma... ma life. But A've actually did a little sales before... em... in fact... A... A did... em... eh sold timeshare, you know. People don't like that. But... eh... ma friend's just back from Marbella and he was only there a fortnight an he was invited over there with friends of his and they... own a timeshare office an things like that... um. An he went off for a holiday, an he was there one day an he closed a deal an he made eighteen hundred poun. He was only there one day! Ye know... so... eh... A was speakin tae him last night... he just cam back last night an he was tellin me, you know, [that] he made... eh... all in, in the f... the... the two... two weeks he was there he made... eh... two thousan nine hundred pouns. For two weeks, you know, an there was only a couple of deals he closed. So that's got my... my brain gaun ye know. Do A want to do that? [...] Certainly, c'mon, if it's gonna be that kind o money – definitely, that's for me.*

*em... A went over for a holiday. A went over for... for a month tae begin with but em... A got tae know the... the the jet set as... as they would call thirsels.*4 *An A actually got caught up in it an... an started drivin a car for this... this fella, [A] was doin an OPC – an Outer Personal Contact, tae get people off the street to... to get them into the hard-line sellers in the resorts. An he was payin me... em, like five hundred pouns a week – cash, ye know. So, that kinda... was a... played a... a major part of me stayin for six months ye know (laugh).*
Well... the... the... there's... there is dirty tactics... if... if... for want of a better word. Em... on the high... on the... the... the line, actually selling, they have to let people know what they're gettin an what it... what obviously... have the the bare essentials... what... what they're gettin... em... how it is a saving, they're gettin this for a saving an... what

---

they're gettin it for, and can ye afford it? An the... the...
one of the dirtiest tricks is ... eh... A... A didn't like it at all,
was... em... there would be lots o... em... contact with the
woman, speakin tae the woman an... an have the... the
husban(d) sittin kinda quiet. But the... it was mostly... eh...
their spiel[5] was mostly directed at the woman, ye know.
The hard line seller would actually *embarrass* them into
buying somethin, buyin a timeshare. 'So ye can't afford that,
as yer base bracket does... doesn't meet this criteria then?'
And the wife would go to the husband, 'Of course. You tell
him. Of course it wid.' Ye know. 'We can afford this.' 'So ye
can afford it? Sign here.' That was one of the dirty tricks an
A didn't like that at all, ye know. Embarrassin people intae
actually spendin their money...

I employ... mostly... eh... joviality... the... let them know
that... that... that Am not a robot, ye know, an actually
have a personality... But em A try to be as honest as A pos-
sibly can. Ye know, if... if... if A'm actually selling a product –
A have tae believe in that first, ye know. If A know A'm
givin people a deal... that'll make me feel em... ten times
better in ma work. Actually gettin people to buy, you know.

CA: *You were saying that... eh sometimes, you know, when
you're... eh... gettin enthusiastic on the phone...*

CHARLIE: *Over-enthusiastic...*

CA: *Well te... te... tell me [you were just] what you were...*

CHARLIE: *Well... em... when A do actually feel Ave got a...
a... a sale happening, A kinna run off, an it's very evident
that A... A'm excited ye know an it's... eh... whoever A'm
speakin tae at the other end o the phone – my 'fish' as
they... we would call them – ... em... they would notice that,
ye know, and say, 'What's the catch here? This guy's too
excited,' ye know.*

[... ly] the whole office knew I was... a... a there was a
deal happening because everybody in... in the office as as
well as down the corridor in the other offices, they could
hear me, ye know. So this is me tryin tae be polite tae this
guy callin him Rab an he was on eh... he was on a mobile
phone in his car, with his window down. He's askin me tae

---

[5]   prepared speech, sales pitch.

*speak up, ye know an that's the worst thing you could say
tae me wh... when I['m] think I've got a sale happenin, ye
know an I'm bloody... I'm away o... off it an... a... as it is an
he's askin me tae speak up so it's 'Yes Rab' ye know, an
people could pr... probably hear me in Govan[6]... ye know.
[Aye.] That was very funny that day. [And] I put the phone
back down, everybody in the office [who's wi us] startit
clappin ye know. A was... 'Ye done well there Charlie.
(Laughs) Ye done well there!'*

Points to notice in Charlie's Glasgow

He is a rather self-conscious, careful speaker and often deliberately
avoids less socially acceptable dialect features eg *saving* [se:vɪŋ]
rather than using the [ɪn] suffix which seems more natural to him
and he also sometimes almost over-pronounces /t/ where he is
consciously avoiding the glottal stop: *a little sales, ten times better.*

In fact he code-drifts between his higher register sales-patter
and his more relaxed conversational register. This code-drifting is
a common feature of Glaswegian speech. However, there is no
weakening in his distinctive Glasgow intonation pattern. Charlie
demonstrates this pattern particularly well towards the end of the
extract.

Consonants

1. Although Charlie sometimes avoids the glottal stop, it is obviously his most natural option for /t/.

2. He simplifies the /nd/ consonant cluster to /n/ in *poun, thousan,
pouns, husban* and in most occurrences of *and.*

3. Good examples /l/ being realised as [o] are to be heard in *little,
people.*

Vowels

Charlie has a definite Glasgow drawl. He has marked lengthening
of long vowels (as predicted by the Scottish Vowel Length Rule)
and even some vowels which would be short in other Scots accents
are sometimes lengthened in association with a rising intonation.

1. WATER
/a/ is used after /w/ in the first occurrence of *want.*

2. FAIR
/e/ before /r/ varies from a very Glasgow [ɛ:r] in the first

---

6   district of Glasgow, by the River Clyde.

occurrence of *timeshare* and most occurrences of *there* to an SSE [e:r] in the second occurrence of *timeshare*.

3. CAT

He has a front /a/ in *car, cash, criteria* etc.

4. COT, CAUGHT

There is little sign of any raising of /ɔ/ except in *afford* where there is [o].

Words to listen to

want, little, timeshare, there, tellin, gaun, people, afford, joviality, product, over-enthusiastic, office.

Tracey

An he's Rangers daft ma daddy. An he's got the wee yin[7] a... no that I agree wi it or anythin but he's got the wee yin, 'Oh who's the best,' ye know, 'Who's the best... Rangers!' an... ah... awful... but it's quite a problem because... ma dad's a Rangers supporter ye know an that's associated wi the Protestant religion in Glasgow... an if ye're a Celtic supporter, ye're a Catholic. It's not true, right? Because some people are Celtic supporters and they're Protestants... they go to church or whatever, they don't go tae chapel or whatever. But Peter's a Celtic supporter an a Catholic an I'm n... not anythin but I'm a Protestant so... how do... whit dae ye... how do get round that... ye know, when ye're gonnae get married... tae this person? So I've spoke tae ma dad an he says, 'Ye [can] get married anywhere hen[8]... don't get married in a chapel.' An I say 'Right, dad, OK.' So... he widnae be there if I married in a chapel... but eh... him an Pete – they get on great, they love each other. It's... it's brilliant. But it's a huge thing in Glasgow, football. Football's a huge thing.

Things to note in Tracey's Glasgow

1. There is voicing of /t/ to /d/ in *Protestant*.

2. Note the glottal stop and running together of go *to* as [goʔe].

3. *Huge* has a closing up of the glide so that [hjʉdʒ] becomes more like [hʃʉdʒ].

4. Initial *th-* /θ/ is replaced with /h/ in *thing*.

---

[7] one (another Glasgow form of this numeral is *wan*)

[8] familiar form of address to a girl or woman

Nan

NAN: *Do you know I got... my mother sent me to elocution lessons when A wis about seven and A went tae... eh this woman in Kirk[lee] Street, right, and she she had me sayin aw this rubbish. Anywey. An then they had this big exhibition an A'd tae say this poem an go up on this stage an A wis staunnin[9] (th)ere. A wis shakin. You should have heard me. A cannae even mind[10] the poem noo. Sometimes it comes back to me. And (th)en years later ma mother... A was... we were talkin an my mother went 'Tae think A actually peyed hauf a croon an hoor tae get you eh, you know, elocution!' A used to be all right for about two hoors after A came oot. See efter that. That was it. It wis hauf a c... Two and six an hour at that time. Am no... Am no gien away ma age, that was what it was.*

JACKIE: *Victoria's heid wis on the back o it as well. (laugh)*

NAN: *Naw, it wisna Victoria. A wisnae... Am not that old. (laugh)*

CA: *So you used to go to Rothesay for your... [holidays]?*

NAN: *Oh we loved it, ay. She'll remember aw that daen't ye? She... we used to go wi ma Ma and Archie. An it was in this room wi the weans an A was in this bed recess an this... Oh mind! One time A got sunburnt. We went tae that [whit dae ye...] Kilchattan Bay.*

DI: *How d'ye get sunburnt at Ro(th)esay?*

NAN: *A did. A got roastit.*

DI: *In the photographs everybody's got their coats on [...]*

NAN: *Ah, but A... A'd a bikini on. A bought this bikini, right. It wis a royal blue an white stripe an A thought A wis the cat's whiskers. An A'm lyin at... that wis when you didnae use... [I mean] you couldn' afford the oil. Nobody ever mentioned the oil or any cream or anyhin for yer legs. Huh! Nae wonder they're aw wrinkles the day.[11] An A wis lyin at Kilchattan Bay an the weans are aw playin aboot. That wis aw right [ye jist got up] That's us. We'll aw go home. See that night! My knees wouldnae bend. Ma legs*

---

[9] standing

[10] remember

[11] today

were absolutely roasted. A couldnae get intae bed. A'd tae
sit wi ma legs hingin oot the bed, d'you remember? No
you'll no remember, you were only a wee lassie.

DI: [I don't remember...]

NAN: [Goin like that... do remember.] Ma legs! Oh A wis only
a [wee] young lassie at the time. But oh did A suffer. Let me
tell... That wis just nae oil. A've never... A don't think A've
ever sunbathed since. A wis absolutely that colour. Ma legs
an ma belly right across (th)ere. An A thought A wis gonnae
look like a film star. [...]

JACKIE: It was a la... Children's Corner as well, Carol Ann.
That was the size o Chil... Children's Corner. Right? For all
the... the weans that was in Rothesay. It was a battle to go
on the beach. Wasn't it?

DI: The beach was tiny, wasn't it?

JACKIE: An' that was Children's Corner!

NAN: Ay, mind the tide... the tide used to come in an ye
moved yer deck chair and if ye fell asleep ye felt yer feet
gettin wet the tide was so near yer feet.

JACKIE: Three weans and the beach was full. (laughs)

NAN: Do you remember [but... the...] ma granny an aw
them they used to all come doon for the weekend, right?
[Jackie that] do you re... mind them aw comin doon for
the weekend and they all went to the pub... that Tony's,
an The Black Bull and aw that? So A had the weans. So A
had to walk aboot Ro(th)esay wi the weans on a Setturday
night an they were aw in the pubs and A used tae [go in an
go... like that (beckons). Yous comin? An they'd go like that
(No).] Know where A spent ma Setturday nights? Sittin in
front o [the] Salvation Army an gien them a caramel for
singin (Jackie laughs). See when I think aboot it noo? Aw
the Setterday nights in Ro(th)esay, on ma holidays staunnin
at the Salvation Army, waitin on them aw comin oot o
Tony's pub to go up the road an make them aw tea. I'd go
like that noo! (rude gesture) C'est la vie! Oh God forgive
me, right.

An one night A went to the bingo an A won, never won
anything in ma life, right? Old Auntie Susie was there,

mind? Archie's Auntie Susie? And A won twenty-four poun
an A wis wi ma Auntie Margaret and eh she shouted 'Bingo!
Bingo!' and A was goin 'What is it?' She went 'Ye've won,
ye've won!' an A didnae even know. A went 'Oh, have A
won? Right.' An A jumped off the seat... the seat fell. It was
thon[12] widden seats, (laugh) [An A went tae] sat back
doon... and I sat... I was that excited sat on the flair. So then
A gets ma twenty-four poun an we rins away hame... and
A... there wis Auntie Susie, there wis the weans, there wis
oor Betty, A don't know how many wis in, an A wis gien
them aw two poun each. An A... an A gied Auntie Susan
two poun, an everybody two poun and A got... an A got
to the end an A went like that (looks at empty hand).
DI: You'd no(t)hing left?
NAN: A'd a poun! [Only had] a poun! Ah naw, A had...
A'd gied Auntie Susie a poun because by the time that she
was at the end, A'd gied everybody two poun an aw that
an A got... By the time A got to her, A went 'If A gie her
two poun A'm no gettin anything,' an A gied her a poun.
A got a poun oot ma twenty-four poun!
JACKIE: Twenty-four poun was a lot o money then.
NAN: Oh, [it wis].
JACKIE: Ay, ye sent yer food hamper on before ye cause that
was...
DI: Ye couldnae carry it... (laugh)
JACKIE: Ay, ye couldnae carry it. (laugh)
NAN: That was right.
CA: So, I mean it would be everything you would need for...
NAN: Oh ay, aw... aw your tinned stuff so that you widnae
buy [it] because then... that was luxury goin on holiday.
DI: So was there nae shops in Ro(th)esay?
JACKIE: Ay.
NAN: Ay but you were in a club...
DI: They'd put the prices up because it was the Glasgow
Fair...
JACKIE: They put the prices up because o the Glasgow Fair,
right?

---

[12] those

NAN: *An then you joined a club an aw that. That's what she's sayin...*

JACKIE: *An Cu... Curley's,*[13] *ye know. So ye got... ye didnae take butter or anyhing like that. Ye took tins like tinned meat an aw that that and ye just b... an ye went tae the field and ye stole (th)e... potatoes oot the field doon in Ro(th)esay so you didn't need to buy, ye know. And there were always a lovely wee bakers [at the co...]. Mind that, we steyed up a close that made coffins?*

NAN: *Oh...*

JACKIE: *Oh my God! A hears this knock knock knock knockin [on wid]. I goes, 'What the blazes is that [for at this time]? See when A [went oot] an aw the coffins are aw stacked up (laugh). Noo A'm talkin about a hamper nearly the size o this settee. Right? Because ye never knew when ye were gettin visitors and aw that. An the like, the last... the top... on the top o the hamper every year went the... the... the Wellingtons and the... the yella raincoats and the hats.*

NAN: *Ye had to have yer rail ticket. Ye had to buy yer rail ticket to get your hamper [em] tae take your hamper. So ye'd buy yer rail ticket in advance. So one time A was kin(d)a short an A had to get the hamper away cos it was up to here wi weans' claes.*[14] *So A went up and A got wan rail ticket because A couldnae buy the two, right? So any- wey we were goin wur holidays and that and A kept sayin 'A'll get a ticket an that. A'll get a ticket next... A'll get it the morra'.*[15] *A never went for another ticket. So, we were goin wur holidays an we got through in the train an we got aff at Wemyss Bay and [then we're] gettin on the boat, an James wis in the pram at the time an A only had wan ticket an A never telt big John. He was a right big quiet soul, he would never hae done hauf the things, you know? An we got tae the boat. We were on the train and the man came to collect the tickets, that's what it wis. And A went like that. (beckons) 'John.' You know? He came oot o his seat. A went like that. 'Ave only got wan ticket. You go for a walk and A'll go for a walk wi [...].' Oh... he nearly had*

---

[13] chain of small grocers

[14] children's clothes

[15] tomorrow

a bad turn, [an a says... an A went]... 'Don't cause a
commotion. A've only wan ticket an that's it.' He went,
'Well, A'm steyin wi the weans,' he says. Eh. So A gied him
the ticket. So A was walkin about the train... eh... past the
collector. [A went], 'Hello. How ye doin?' an that. And then
A was goin like that, 'Gie me the ticket noo'. An He's goin
like that, 'No way. [He] punched the ticket' and he's just
goin 'You'll jist take yer consequences,' an aw this. So we
get aff the train an (th)at was nae bother, done that...
an I thought this was [... laughin]. I didnae think it was
[... didnae think anythin o it]. We gets aff the train an we're
gettin on the boat, wi the pram an the weans an cases.
An the hamper had... was already on but, [know,] this,
like bags an things. An I went like that tae the man that
was takin the tickets, 'Scuse me sir, 'scuse me. Would you
help me up?' Big John went on wi the... the other two.
Right? 'Scuse me, could you help me wi this buggy?' A was
in the bag ye know [an aw that] (pretends to rummage,
head down, in a bag). He went, 'Nae bother', lifts it up the
boat. 'Nae bother hen. There ye go.' A went, 'Thank you'.

Things to note in Nan's Glasgow

This extract starts with an interesting sociolinguistic point. Just why
was Nan sent to elocution lessons? She switches easily, if satirically,
into SSE: *two and six an hour*, demonstrating the ability and readi-
ness of Glasgow speakers to move rapidly in and out of regional
dialect in response to social context. This code-switching, like the
elocution lessons, indicates an association, on the speaker's part,
between lower social status and regional dialect forms of speech.

Intonation

The main speaker, Nan, is a particularly energetic raconteuse. Her
speech is so rapid and fluent that words are sometimes very lightly
articulated or glossed over. She uses a wide range of pitch in the
typically Glasgow 'scoop and rise' pattern, and her use of vowel
length for emphasis is particularly striking:

> *haufa croon an hoor*
> *absolutely roastit*
> *ma belly*

Even when she speaks French, the Glasgow intonation remains:
Cest la vie.

Consonants

1. Nan provides plenty of examples of glottal stops or marked glottalisation.

years later   *aw right*   *A'm no that old*

2. Her voiceless dental fricative /θ/ becomes /h/ in *cream or anyhin*. This particular speaker only does this in the word *anyhin*.

3. The voiced dental fricative /ð/ becomes a tap [ɾ] in *mother > morrer/morr* and in many of the occurrences of *the*, eg *the morra > ra morra*. It is particularly well marked in *nae bother > nae borrer*.

4. This extract offers examples of TH-deletion in *Ro(th)esay, claes, wi*.

5. Nan regularly simplifies /nd/ to /n/ as you can hear in most occurrences of *and* as well as in *staunnin* and *poun*.

6. The [o] quality of /l/ when it stands as a syllable on its own can be heard when Jackie says *battle*.

7. The blade or front of the tongue (rather than the tip) may be used for /s/. This is clearest in *A wis staunnin there*.

Vowels

1. FAIR

The distinctively Glasgow [ɛ:] is found in *Glasgow Fair, deck chair* although her pronunciation of *there* shows a degree of variation.

2. COT, CAUGHT

The SSE /ɔ/ is nearly always raised to /o/ and this may become more noticeable in association with lengthening *Children's Corner* [ko:rnər], *on ma holidays, coffins*.

3. Where /l/ is lost *all > aw* [ɔ:].

4. Where /l/ is not lost *full* rhymes with *dull* [fʌɬ] but the name of the pub, *The Black Bull* keeps the SSE [buɬ] in this extract.

5. Notice the [ɔ] vowel in *staunnin*.

6. *Film* has an extra vowel [fɪɬəm].

Words to listen to

anywey, staunnin, mother, actually, peyed, hauf, held, daen't, sunburnt, Ro(th)esay, roastit, film, Corner, battle, full, Setturday, caramel, staun(d)in, Susie, widden, flair, Betty, poun(d), gied, food, hamper, Fair, aw, close, coffins, buy, holidays, telt, steyin, consequences, nae borrer.

EDINBURGH

The main features of the Edinburgh accent are also found in the adjacent Midlothian area, including Dalkeith, Penicuik and Bonnyrigg, and the accents of East Lothian are closely related. As in Glasgow, the proportion of SSE to dialect forms increases with social status and formality. Code-switching is common.

Intonation

The range of pitch is less varied in Edinburgh than in Glasgow. The tune is generally falling but rises with questions. There is a variable degree of rise with tags such as the distinctively Edinburgh *like* and *ye ken*. Stress is indicated primarily by an increase in volume, rather than by the variation in pitch which characterises Glasgow. Sean and Christie are good examples of Edinburgh intonation: it might help to think of them as sounding like revving motorcycles or an express train going 'over-the-points, over-the-points'. The pattern could be described as a low plateau with either a dip or a rise at the end of a phrase.

Mouth Position

The tongue is slightly back in the mouth so that the vowels are generally retracted. It may help to imagine the voice being 'focused' on the arch of the hard palate. Lips are relaxed and the jaw position is quite close so that some vowels show slight raising.

Consonants

1. Edinburgh shares several of its consonant features with Glasgow:
a)   The glottal stop is very often completely or partially substituted for /t/.
b)   In *something*, *nothing* etc, /θ/ may lose its dental quality and become [h] or the voiceless equivalent of the next consonant.
c)   /ð/ may be realised as a tap [ɾ] at the start of words or between vowels. Sean provides a good example of this, *brother > brorr*.
d)   After vowels or where it forms a syllable on its own in words like *bottle*, *people*, *little*, /l/ may be realised as [o].
2. A consonantal feature which is peculiar to Edinburgh is the assimilation in initial /tr-/ and /θr-/ clusters, making *tree* sound like *(t)shree* and *three* sound like *shree*. What seems to be happening here with the /r/ is that the voice is being switched on late following the voiceless consonants. The tongue is at the back of, or just

behind, the alveolar ridge and the nearest voiceless sound that the ear recognises, for this first part of the /r/, is /ʃ/, the palatal, voiceless fricative in *ship* etc.

3. Particularly in younger, lower class speakers, the /ʍ/ sound is disappearing and is being replaced with /w/ so that *which* and *witch* sound identical. Also /x/ is occasionally replaced by /k/ so that *loch* and *lock* become the same. The speakers who do this tend to be working class. They do it whether they are being formal or not and therefore it is not an attempt to sound more like RP. Those speakers who have the older pronunciations tend to have strong views about the 'correctness' of /ʍ/ and /x/.

Vowels

Edinburgh generally lacks the extended vowel length so characteristic of Glasgow, although the /ɛ/ vowel often shows some lengthening. Vowels are a little further back in keeping with the slightly retracted Edinburgh mouth posture.

1. COT, CAUGHT

Some of our speakers, especially Jennie and Sean, show a strong tendency to raise /ɔ/ vowels to /o/ so that *dock* [dɔk] becomes *doak* [dok].

2. BOOT

/ʉ/ is usually used for words such as *poor, boot, cool, school* as well as *out, house, down* where these are pronounced in the Scots manner.

3. BIT

/ɪ/ is usually lowered and retracted. In extreme cases it becomes almost like /ʌ/.

4. BAIT

/e/ is a little higher in Edinburgh than in Glasgow.

5. CAT

/a/ is the vowel which best reflects the Edinburgh mouth posture, (think: arch of the palate) but occasionally tends towards a back [ɑ(:)], even with a hint of lip-rounding, when followed by /n/, /f/, /p/, /k/, /x/ or a glottal stop. Jennie sometimes does this in *flat, black*. A following /l/ may have a similar effect but this is less noticeable in Edinburgh.

6. FEAR, BEAR

/i / and /e/ may be followed by a /ə/ vowel especially before /r/.

Diphthongs

1. TIME

In words like *time, tide* the diphthong is pronounced in Edinburgh as in SSE /ʌi/, perhaps with some raising and fronting of the first element. Where the Scots Vowel Length Rule predicts a long vowel [aːe] is used, *try, tied*.

2. HOUSE

SSE [ʌu] remains unchanged except that younger Edinburgh speakers are fronting the second element so that the resulting diphthong is [ɛʉ].

3. BOY

SSE [ɔe] may have its first element raised, as happens with the monophthong, so that we get [oe].

The pronouns *I* and *my* are *A* and *ma*.

The negative particle in *cannae, dinnae* etc is [ne].

The vowel in <aw> words *braw, snaw* and after loss of /l/ in *a(ll), ba(ll)* is /ɔː/.

The vowel of final *-ly* in *lovely* is [e].

The final vowel in *barrow/barrae, window/windae* is [e].

Of is reduced to [o].

Christie

A 'strag' was somebody that offered theirsel up for a job in Leith Docks, ken,[1] a strag. A 'weekly' was a man that was employed weekly. A 'staff man' was on the books. A fill-the-joug[2] was a... probably a lodgin hoose bird who, tae get a job, would pey for the drink for one of the foremen. Fill-the-joug. So A had my faither eh couldnae get a job because he wisnae a fill-the-joug, [ye know].

The foremen used to stand in the middle maybe they had a... a man with them or no, they used to stand in the middle and roond aboot them was a ring o men c... c... sort o climbin [aw] ower each others' shoulders and everythin like that, their hands outstretched tryin to get a... metal disc which was a job, see. Now that would entitle them maybe to work fae eight o'clock til twelve. That was aw, ken. Sometimes they started at six in the mornin and could get peyd aff at eight, ken. That that was... but it got... a Monday mornin in particular, that got them a stamp. So on a Monday mornin ootside Leith Dock gates, there wiz foremen wi aw their different stances, ken. They [e... lot] had their separate places where they went... and... to start men, and there were thousands o men, thousands and thousands o men, and ma faither used to be in that. And I used to walk doon tae ma work wi... ah... our place was in what ye cawed Tomato Row, it was a row o huts just inside the Dock gates an I had ma... to make my way through thay[3] thousands o men.

An you know the first thing A had to do when A got into the Dock gates, into the comparative peace and quiet o the Docks itsel? Was look at my heels and the bottom of my trousers for spittins and things. [That they... eh... y]... you'd no idea, what it was like. It was really, it was really degradin in the extreme. Well eventually, they started

---

[1] know, commonly used as a tag question in Edinburgh
[2] jug or pint measure
[3] those

a new scheme and outside our row o offices, about a road's breadth away, they built a platform wi a... a... a banisters along the front of the platform facin our offices and the foreman went up... up steps onto this platform, see, and the... the dockers were outside oor offices, and thousands o them, on a Monday particularly. Thousands of them on a Monday. And it was like a slave market. These foremen some of them were... dinnae forget, some of them never paid for a drop you know. A've seen them fawin off the stool in the Central Bar, cos A took a drink masel and well A'd maybe go into the pub at the fit o the Walk[4] on ma road hame and... and there's some o them fawin off their stool these foremen, you know, they... they... they used to go, 'You! You! You an aw!' ken, and these men all fightin and [jorrin] for... for a job. It was like what I imagine what a slave market was like. It was scandalous! To think that men had to face these conditions.

Things to note in Christie's Edinburgh

This is an older, quite conservative speaker (unfortunately, sitting in a creaky chair).

Christie is a very good example of Edinburgh intonation patterns. He has a comparatively level pitch with a dip at the end of utterances. This is so regular that the intonation is very like a revving motorcycle.

Consonants

1. He has frequent substitution or partial substitution of glottal stops for /t/.

2. His /l/ in *middle* is tending towards [o].

3. He frequently has a tap [ɾ] substituted for an initial /ð/, eg *the first thing I had to do, some o* **them**.

Vowels

1. The vowel length is as predicted by the Scottish Vowel Length Rule.

2. BOOT, OOT

He has a strongly rounded [ʉ] in *joug, hoose, roond, aboot* etc.

3. BIT

/ɪ/ is lowered and retracted *infill, drink, six* etc.

---

4   Leith Walk

4. BUT

/ʌ/ is low in *bird, word, hut* etc.

5. BAIT

/e/ is noticeable higher than in Glasgow: *slave* is a very clear example, also *faither, places, degradin* etc.

6. CAT

/a/ is retracted as in *staff, stamp, start* etc.

7. COT, CAUGHT

Christie shows some raising of /ɔ/ towards [o] in *job, morning* etc, but this feature is much more clearly demonstrated by Sean and Jenny. *Of* is heard as [o].

Words to listen to

He has a lot of general Scots features such as the pronunciation of

theirsel, ludgin-hoose, pey, faither, couldnae, roond, cawed, itsel, fawin, masel, fit (foot), hame.

He has a lot of SSE words which illustrate how you can use SSE with the local mouth position:

weekly, bird, hands, particular, stances, thousands, work, Tomato, platform, slave.

Listen for the Edinburgh pronunciation of *used.*

Maureen

A was brought up in... the Heart of Midlothian actually, in Edinburgh, in the Royal Mile between the castle and the palace. A was one o thirteen o a family which was first up best dressed, A'm afraid. If you got up early in the mornin you got the best o the clothes (laugh)... em... what can A say? There was eight girls, five boys, ten o us survived, seven girls and three boys and one brought the other one up because my mum constantly worked a the time and so did my dad. That didna mean we were neglected because she cooked at night and... washed and scrubbed shoes and things during the night and we were never, we never went withoot. We really didnae go withoot. Maybe because A was the last end o the family, like A was the eleventh child and by the time A was growing up some of my brothers and sisters were workin.

The girls, they had to... they were told to go into factories. They weren't allowed to do anything else.

My sister had done commercial at school, typing and things like that. But women werenae allowed to do that, in ma mother's eyes. Ye had to keep the house, for at least a year when you left school, an you had to run it. You got the hou... the money; you had to do the cookin, the cleanin, the washin, the ironin for aw these people and you didnae work, and every one o my sisters had to do that, but Am afraid, as my dad nicknamed named me, 'rebel without a cause' came along and A went out and got mysel a job an A was terrified to tell them that A had one, and A sat there for ages and my dad knew there was something wrong wi us you know, and he's sayin to me, 'You've got somethin on your mind so you might as well say it because, no matter what, you're gonnae have to say it anyway so get it over [wi].' And A told him A had got a job in a printin... printers and he... told ma mother who wore a hearin aid and when you seen the hearin aid gettin switched off you know the han(d)s were coming, (laughter) And no... anyway it didn't get switched off it got turned up. So that meant she was gonnae listen, and she turned round and A mean aw these sisters in front o me, [how many] did A have, A'd Mary, Ellen, Rita, Cathie, four of them, and one sister has now been keepin the house for... six years because there was only one child between us, one was lost, and that was a brother so he didnae keep the hoose. He wasnae allowed to wash a teaspoon. He was out workin and Cathie was waitin on me leavin school to take over because my mother had three jobs. She could earn more than us to keep us. So, Cathie had to stay on, workin, in the house. Keepin the house for six years, A mean she was 21 when she first got a job. It was a nightmare, A mean it was terrible, an A had looked at her and thought no... for...

A don't [know] care what happens to me and it's no for me. It's no my life. So A got this job as a printer and A told my mother, and aw that time that my sister had been doin that... my mother turned roond and laughed and said 'A wondered which one. I might have known it would be you.'

Things to note in Maureen's Edinburgh
Intonation

Again a bit like a revving motorcycle. She speaks in short bursts with heavy stress at the beginning of each phrase. This may be exaggerated by her slight breathing difficulties.

Consonants

Maureen uses quite a lot of glottal stops, there is a hint of reduction of the /θ/ in *something on your mind*, and there is simplification of the /nd/ cluster in *han(d)*.

Vowels

BOOT, OOT

She has quite a rounded [ʉ] in *hoose, roond* etc. The vowel in *school* however, is lower and unrounded so that it sounds more like *skill*.

Words to listen to

early, family, withoot, didnae, werenae, school, aw, workin, years.

Sean

When I was younger it was a great place because we had the beach. I mean it wasnae like Wester Hailes which, you know, it's away out in the middle of naewhere. You had the beach, so, like, ye know, like the summer nights like it is now you'd go doon there and it would be just a big massive adventure like, you know. And you used to have cut doon the... the golf course an chorry⁵ aw the sort o golf baws.

So Muirhouse was great and there used to be Silverknowes which was the sort of private place and... eh... we used to go what we used to call 'chicken runs' like you know and ye sort o just sort o nashed⁶ through their gardens like, ye know, and knock over their plant pots. It was dead innocent stuff. It wasn't like breakin and enterin. It wisnae like, you know, graffiti. It was like, you know. We felt at the time it was really bad like, you know. Course I remember when Safeways got... got built like, ye know, years ago. We were still quite young like, ye know.

---

⁵   steal

⁶   ran, rushed

It was this big massive supermarket like, ye know. I
remember one godforsaken efternoon when we all went
up and my twin brother Kevin was wi me an... em.
There was these guys who were like the mafiosi o
Muirhouse Terrace, like. I say, mafioso, but it really, like,
you know. It was nothin like what it is noo. But... em...
at the time they were big like and so we went up one
Setterday efternoon an a remember we went in an we we
chorried... we chorried aw thay Smarties like, you know
an A had the nerve to go up to the woman and say 'Hey
missus, ye no got any Smarties left?' like efter bein in for
the tenth time and her sort of rushin out to the back you
know. 'We'll just see if there's any Smarties in stock' like,
you know.

But A remember comin oot and thinkin 'aw we've we've
chorried too much now like, you know. They've seen our
faces. They ken us like, you know.' An... em... A remember
sayin to Kevin, my brother Kevin, 'Listen, dinnae go back in.'
We've got this big stockpile at the back o Safeways car park
like you know by the railway embankment, ye know. Enough
tae... enough sweeties tae... an Smarties, to survive for a
week. A remember turnin away an then turnin roon an
Kevin had went in an A thought 'Aw no,' like. A just had
this awful feelin he was goin to get nabbed like, you know.
An... em... he did and A remember sittin waitin an waitin
for him to come oot an he didnae come oot an the big
terrifying thing aboot it was my old man, my dad. He was
off that day. Ma dad was a seaman like, you know and eh
A'm no tryin to sa ... If my mum found us she would be a
lot mair sortae like you know wise[7] aboot it. She wouldnae
let ma dad ken. She'd gie us a good whack aroond the ear
wi a dishcloth like you know an sort us out like, but ma dad
would just he would just... just murder us like, you know.
An A [A've] waited an A waited and A thought 'Oh A've
got to go into the shop. A've got to go in and see what's
happened here' and A sortae went in like, you know,
thinkin A was going to get grabbed at any minute and
A could just see my brother Kevin's heid, just above the

---

7   sane, sensible

wee bit where they all sortae sit. There was this wee box bit that they sit like ye know, and do all their sort ae like ye know tillin up and stuff like that and A saw his wee heid up there and A went, 'Aw no'. And then A sort o nashed oot the shop like you know because the guys were lookin at me like you know the staff like, you know, thinkin, 'he must be one of them as well', and A came oot like you know and A remember Kevin my brother gettin into the ... gettin in to the... eh... the police car an that and A had to walk hame and it was the longest walk hame like you know, draggin my heels thinkin Kevin would [...]... A mean... first thing my da, my old man would have said, he would have said, 'Where's Sean?' ye know because we were always together when we were younger like, you know. And A remember where we lived. It was Muirhouse Terrace an there wis like three big sort ae maisonette blocks like, you know an in the centre there was this sort o waste ground where we had bonies which was like bonfires like, you know and eh. Burnt oot patch in the middle of this grass like you know. An A remember sort o like, [ye know] wi the rest of them standin, eh the ones that didnae get caught, ye know, and A could feel ma dad ma... ma... ma neck bein burnt by ma dad's like eyes like oot the hoose window like, you know and as A turned roond and looked up like, you know he just the way he like threw the windae open like, you know an he was almost like balancin over his knees. 'Sean, get up here noo!' like, ye know. A just went, 'Aw no' and that was it like, you know, climbin up the stair going, 'Aw now that's it' and A went in you know cos and Kevin's nae[where] to be seen like. He was downstairs like you know in his bedroom like you know greetin,[8] like, you know. He'd just had a good tannin like. 'Where hae ye been?' 'But... but... but... but... but.' Smash! Like, you know. That was it. Oot wi the belt [...] that was it you know. God! Couldnae sit doon for a week like.

---

[8] crying

Things to note in Sean's Edinburgh

Intonation

Sean's intonation is the typical Edinburgh revving bike. It is most obvious when he is at his most animated.

Consonants

1. Sean has a very high proportion of glottal stops to /t/.
2. He clearly demonstrates the use of a tap [ɾ] between vowels in *brother>brorr*.
3. In *whack*, and *naewhere* the /ʍ/ usually found in Scottish speech has been replaced with [w] in this younger speaker.

Vowels

1. His vowels lengths are as predicted by the Scottish Vowel Length Rule. Notice the lengthened vowels before /r/ in *Smarties*, *carpark* and word finally in *dae(in)*. It is easy to hear the lengthened [ɛ:] before the voiced fricative /v/ in *Kevin*.
2. CAT

His /a/ is often quite far back, even tending towards [ɑ], in *grass, grabbed, nashed* etc.
3. COT, CAUGHT

There is some, usually only slight, raising of /ɔ/ but some words show very marked raising to [o] as in *off, shop*. The /o/ vowel in the tag, *ye know*, is lowered to /ɔ/ when unstressed.
4. BOOT, OOT

His [ʉ] in *oot, won, noo* etc is strongly rounded.
5. BAIT

/e/ is higher than in Glasgow: *Safeways, away* etc.
6. BIT

/ɪ/ is lowered: *in, bit, big* etc.

Diphthongs

TIME

Sean provides a good contrast between the short diphthong [ʌi] in *stockpile, like* and the lengthened [a:e] in *guys, wise*.

Words to listen to

Chorry, baws, nashed, Setterday, efternoon, aw, didnae, daein, oot, Kevin, dinnae, won, waitin, off, murder, shop, sortae, held, hame, hoose, windae, doonstairs, greetin, tannin.

Jenny

JENNY: *Oh the coat, that's it. The... the coat, ma... ma Auntie Phemie's coat.*

It was this coat that my Auntie Phemie left us one time and it was a jaiket. Well, she was a stout woman, ken, and there was pockets in this coat and it went right doon. Well it was rare for stealin anythin. Pinchin. Carrot and turnip an aw the rest o it and inside was pockets fae there right doon tae the flair, ken, and A used tae wheel this barrae and it was... it... these great big wheels and A was aye terrified [I'd reco...] that somebody would recognise me, ye ken, wheelin this barrae up the Ferry Road. My grannie used to stey beside us and as I say my grannie didnae like me. She just liked the laddies in the faimlie[9] and it used to annoy me, ken, because eh I used to dae aw the messages[10] for the folk there, an the folk up the stair an aw the rest of it. And it was Liptons in the Kirkgate. It was Liptons and the Buttercup and all these old shops that was up there we used to go... An (th)en was Crawfords.[11] I've got aw these pictures that's in that thingmie – Crawfords. We used to go there for the old chats[12] and the... the every mornin, ken, if when the shop first opened, you used to get the... the bread cheap and the scones and the bit buns. It's the only time we had ever buns, ken, wis frae Crawfords.

JUNE: *The day befores.*

JENNY: *Ay... Ay.*

JENNY: *The black and white funnel was a Currie's boat. An we s... as A say, we... the first flat was offices an the next flat was where we lived. Three windows that wey an three windows that wey and we used to could see across Newcastle sheds where aw the beer barrels were and that was where we used to go climbin up and through the wa and into the... where the beer barrels was. But A used to ken when the boat came in wi the black and white funnel.*

---

[9]   family

[10]   shopping

[11]   chain of bakeries

[12]   morsel, used in Edinburgh in the sense of baker's rejects or leftovers

*A used to dash up the stair to my mother and say, 'The
boat's in.' So A used to go doon and climb through this
railins and thingmie go up there to where the boat left.
And the man always knew me and eh... eh... they had,
ken, they used to buy for the men that worked on the boat.
It was a like a leg o lamb or something like that. Well A
used to go and A used to get the... the leg o lamb, ken,
the bits o bone. But ken... but aye hingin wi meat, ken.
An A used get this and A used to run hame wi it an ma
Ma used to make soup an thingmie. An we aye had a dug,
ken. We were poor but we had a bloody dug.*

    *An there was a crane there that ma grannie had lost
her finger on, years ago. An that was... I telt ye aboot
her finger wi [her] pan drops.*[13] *She... had a finger off...
a thingmie (artificial finger)... ma grannie, this is the
grannie that didnae like me, ken? She used to put her
pan drops in that finger an take ma brothers tae the church
an... keepin feedin them wi pan drops, ken.*

Things to note in Jenny's Edinburgh Consonants

1. Jenny provides an example of the Edinburgh assimilation of
/θr/ so that *three windows* sounds very much like *shree windows*.
Listen, too, for *through (shroo) the wa* and *through (shroo) the
railins*.

2. She often uses the glottal stop as a complete or partial substitute
for /t/.

3. She has an example of a tap [ɾ] realisation of /ð/ in *mother*.

4. The first time she says *finger* there is no /g/ sound so that it
rhymes with *singer*.

Vowels

1. COT, CAUGHT: Jenny has a decided preference for a raised
/ɔ/. An [o] sound is used in *pockets, on, lot* etc.

2. BOOT, OOT: She has a well-rounded [ʉ] in *doon, aboot, hoose*.

3. There are examples of final <ow> pronounced as /e/ in *barrow/
barrae* and *followed*.

Words to listen to

    *jaiket, pockets, on, flair, barrae, wisnae, chats, mornin, shop,
scones, dock, through, three, wa(ll), mother, thingmie, lamb,
hingin, hame, dug, followed, pan drops.*

---

[13] mint imperials, also known as grannie sookers

Susie

Well ye... you could start any time you liked in the mornin at the berry pickin. So we used to start about eight o'clock in the mornin. And all go up the drills and get wir... [an]... pick the berries. Well, they told us the berries wis for dyein which I hope because ye didnae get very much for pickin them and to to weigh them we used to pee in the pail. To make more money.

Things to note in Susie's Edinburgh

Beware of raspberries!

Words to listen to

berry, used, dyein.

DUNDEE

Dundee speakers seem confident about using their own dialect and make less conscious effort to move towards SSE than Edinburgh and Glasgow speakers when faced with a microphone and an SSE interviewer. There is very little evidence of code-switching or code-drifting in our speakers.

As you might expect, since Dundee is between Edinburgh and Aberdeen, the accent shares features of both. In fact, Dundee lies on the boundary between the central group of dialects and the northern group. This makes the vowel system particularly interesting.

Intonation

There are no marked variations in pitch although, typically, there is a rise or rise/fall at the end of an utterance. There is, however, variation in stress and when a word is emphasised using stress there is an associated rise in tone.

Mouth Position

The tongue is retracted. It may help to think of 'focusing' the voice on the back of the hard palate but not as far as the soft palate or you will 'swallow' the sound. Lip movement is minimal (you may need to compromise for intelligibility). The mouth position shows up in the /a/ which has a more definite retraction than Edinburgh without reaching the extreme of Aberdeen.

Consonants

1. /r/ is always clearly articulated even occasionally rolled.
2. Consistent with the back mouth position, /l/ is very dark.
3. There are a lot of glottal stops as a variant of /t/. Glottal stops are less common in older speakers.
4. Final devoicing of /d/ may occur as in *retired* [rətɛːrt] (Annie).
5. /nd/ consonant clusters are often simplified to /n/ as in *an(d)*.
6. Loss of /v/ as in *hae, of* and *twel(v)e* is common. In *of* the remaining vowel may be a nondescript central [ə], [a] or [e].
7. There is some TH-dropping as in *wi(th), clae(th)es*.
8. This accent is distinguished from Aberdeen by NOT having frequent loss of initial /ð/ although this does sometimes occur as in Annie's *(th)ere*.

Vowels

1. TIME

a) The distinctive Dundee feature is the substitution of [ɛ:] for the [a:e] diphthong in words like *five* > *fehv, pie* > *peh, buy* > *beh, I* > *Eh, ay, aye* > *eh, retired* > *retehrd*. These are the vowels predicted as long by the Scottish Vowel Length Rule (See SSE). Michael Marra, the Dundee singer/songwriter, reports hearing this sound in words like *Pythagorus* and *Thailand* in the speech of younger Dundonians giving a clear indication of just how vigorous this feature is. Because the [ɛ:] is so striking, there may be a temptation to overdo it. You will hear many exceptions in the recordings. Listening to the recordings, you will notice how easily and naturally it slips in. We have not used <eh> spelling in the transcriptions because it would have made them much harder to read, especially where it caused confusion between the *eh* hesitation and the pronoun *I*.

b) The short vowels are still [ʌi] as in *wifie, times, bridie*.

c) In a small number of words /e/ become a diphthong [ɛi]: *way* > *wey, pay* > *pey, Tay* > *Tey*. This is particularly common after /w/. Annie uses this diphthong with *weyst* (waist). Lengthening takes place as predicted by the Scots Vowel Length Rule to give [ɛ:i].

2. CAT

/a/ is back compared with Glasgow and Edinburgh. This is closer to [ɑ], not quite so far back as an Aberdeen [ɑ], but it is still very noticeable.

3. COT, CAUGHT

Many of the speakers show considerable raising of /ɔ/, even collapsing it with /o/ so that *rod* is pronounced like *road*.

4. HOOSE/MOON

Hoose, moon, put etc all have [ʉ] with some loss of lip rounding but watch out for fronting and unrounding of some <oo> words, like *good/guid* which has [ɪ], or even [i] as is common in Aberdeen. *Do* occasionally falls into this category [di:].

5. OLD

Where Edinburgh and Glasgow have [ɔ(:)] as in *auld, braw, awa, snaw, fa(ll), ba(ll)* etc, Dundee has a more northern [ɑ(:)]. So you hear *aald, braa, awaa, snaa, faa, baa*.

6. BIT

Most occurrences of /ɪ/ are closer to [ʌ].

7. /u/, where the following /l/ is not lost, becomes [ʌ] as *in full* [fʌɬ].

8. /ɛ/ and /e/ are very occasionally raised towards [ɪ]. Although it is not very common, it is worth watching for as it is a good indicator of a Dundee accent. This is one to be used sparingly and only if you are sure it is appropriate. Listen for Annie using the words *pastry, paper and sherry.*

9. WAY

See TIME (c).

10. HOUSE

Some younger speakers are lowering the first part of this diphthong when they select the HOUSE form of words rather than the HOOSE form. Where older speakers have [hʌus], some younger speakers are approaching [haus]. There is a hint of this when Ben says, *It's all arms and legs flappin about.*

The pronouns *I* and *my* are *Eh* and *meh.*
The negative particle in *canna, dinna* is [na].
The vowel in <aw> words braw, snaw and after loss of /l/ in *a(ll), ba(ll)* is [ɑ:].
The vowel of final -*ly* in *lovely* is [ɪ].
The final vowel of *barrow/barrae, window/windae* is [e]
Of is reduced to [ə], [e] or [ɑ].

DUNDEE RECORDINGS

Annie

CR: *What was it like in the mills?*

ANNIE: *Oh hard, aafae hard. Though ye got yaised[1] til[2] it but it was lang hoors. Ye started eight in the mornin ah... tae eight at night but we'd to ging[3] in at seven for to clean the frames. I'd three cl... frames to clean because ye needed the money. Well, ye got a shillin fae each spinner if you cleaned their frames and did their ends. Lang, lang frames. Have you ever seen a frame? It's hard work but you got yaised til it but you worked to Setterday at twel o'clock... and my mother an my sisters worked there an aa. Twa sisters and... eh... they were shifters. My mother was a shiftin wifie.[4]*

There was twa shiftin wifies... eh... in oor place and (th)en there was another twa shiftin wifies ben the hoose[5] and then in the ither place there was another shiftin wifie. There was five or six ower the... in the mill and they aa looked efter the shifters an the piecers, to dae the frames. They blew a whistle an you'd to run like blazes an shift. Ye ken? You'd to put a bag aroond yer... yer waist wi aa the bobbins in it. Big bobbins. Well ye filled that. As soon as ye stopped shiftin, ye come back again and filled aa yer baggie and waited on the next whistle for the frames aa fillin up and the bobbins were f... had to be right full. Well you shifted them an put them in a box and you put empty bobbins on an then you fixed them up an the frame went.

CR: *That must've been heavy work.*

ANNIE: *Oh it was heavy. Nae wonder we were aa... aa marked aroond the stomach. Right bathered wi yer... 'course ye had... ye tied it aroond yer weyst this bag*

---

[1]   used

[2]   to

[3]   go

[4]   woman (the *-ie* suffix is particularly associated with Aberdeen but is not uncommon in Dundee)

[5]   in the interior

and it had to be aye full. Shiftin [was]... Some shiftin wifies
werena bad but other yins were aaffie... oh wicked,
wicked... Some o the wemen were hard, you know.
They... they drunk and they snuffed an they... aa their...
things that they did.

CR: *Did you have any customs at the mill if one of the lassies
was gettin married?*

ANNIE: *Oh Ay. Ye dressed them up an put them in a barrae
and... and had a... a potty, ken, a po, we used tae cry[6]
them. An ye filled it wi sawdust an aathing an put flooers...
ye did [up] that was her bouquet an she cam doon.
Anither ane dressed as... eh... the best maid. And they
dressed them up and... eh... they took them awa doon
the hill and awa fae... the de... the... the... the works
and come awa doon the tap o the hill under the clock
and aa sang and made chainies aroond her and (th)en ye
went up tae their mither's hoose and ye got a cup o tea.
Sometimes ye got a sherry. Other times, oh it begun to
get better as ye got aalder. We went tae ane's and oh
their dresses and aathing were braa.[7] Oh God, ay! An
... eh... took hame in pony an trap. We were aa in this
trap gettin took hame, an the wee pony, whit a shame!
Och, we were aa slim in thay days and we were took awa
hame tae the mither's and, oh God, we got steak pie and
tatties[8] and aathing. Some o them were great but years...
when we were younger it was just a cup o tea, sometimes
a wee shirry, ither times just the... the tea and eh...
eh maybe a pastry that was goin or a bun, anything.
An... but oh, as they begin to get aalder oh it was
swankier.[9] The dresses an aathing. Oh gee! They used
to bring in their ain dresses, whaur afore we used to bring
in aald things oot o the rag store. Used to ging doon to the
rag store and get... eh... rags an mak up things for them an
dress em up and dress up dollies and aathing, ken, when
any o them was expectin.*

---

6   call

7   fine

8   potatoes

9   posher

*An (th)en at the holiday time... ye had... eh... ye aa bunced
up*[10]*... eh... for tae hae something special, get pies an
bridies brought in an eh... a bottle o sherry, cheap sherry.*
CR: *Ay?*
ANNIE: *The shiftin wi... wifie, that was the only day ye were
allowed it. But ye hurried up an got yer work done an sat
doon an ye had yer burst up [...] they cried it.*

*My father worked in em... Gilroys an... at the dye...
[he] went to the dye works. Oh, he worked aa his days.
Hard worker. Must admit. An old crab. He was affie strict.
Couldnae look at a paper. You couldna [...] I mind o gettin
ma ears pierced an a awa wi masel ye see. Sixteen. Fourteen
it was, first. It was a perm an... eh... I just came in aa awa
wi masel because I'd had this five shillinny perm. Saved up
for ten weeks an [a] ken what he did? Come in an put's
under the well.*[11]

*[Of] course he used tae hae big boots. Thon grea(t) big
heavy boots. An he used tae... s... ken if you [were] cheeky
or anything or say onything back ye got it one efter the
other, the boots. An ye daurna move awa until he threw
thay boots. Ye couldna look at my father... I've seen me
makin faces at him an here he'd be lookin in the gless an
he'd see me. We didna get aff wi a thing. Not a thing.
My father just lifted his hand tae ye. But, I mean, mind,
[m]... he wisnae the only yin. A lot o the men were like
that years ago. Jist, whit would ye cry them? Eh... sort ae
cowards. They... lifted their fists. Eh... he was hard.
He lived till he was eighty-three. D'you ken what happened
when he was eighty-three? Eh. Died. He died in Victoria
ho... hospital wi cancer. And... eh... we were up in the hoose
gettin it cleaned. And ma niece was gettin it. And... eh...
my sister says, 'Annie, there's somebody at the door'. An I
went awa tae the door. And this man says, 'Is Mr Broon in?'
An I says, 'My father, Mr Brown?' He says, 'Ay' he says 'I've
got a job on for him an he kens the job, at the dyein.' He
was aafie good at that, ken, pickin the richt dyes an that.
An he says, 'I've got a job on an I... I... I ken that... eh...*

---

[10] saved up a kitty
[11] tap

*he's up in years an that, but ye see, he kens the job.' An ma
sister says, 'D'you ken how aald my father is?' He says, 'No,
he's a guid worker.' An we says we didna ken he was workin
doon at that factory [because] he'd left his work, finished,
[well, I] mean, retired. An... eh... that was him. Money for
drink. An she says, 'Well, news for ye. Ma father was buried
the day.'*[12]

Things to note in Annie's Dundee

Annie shows almost complete resistance to code-shifting. This
remarkable lady is one of our older informants.

Intonation

In spite of being a fluent and animated speaker, her intonation is
very flat, with only slight rises or falls at the end of utterances.

Mouth position

She has the back position typical of Dundee.

Consonants

Although there are a quite a few glottal stops used as alternatives
to /t/, there are not as many as a younger speaker would have and
her glottalisation is often only partial. The frequency of the glottal
stop is often quite a good guide to age.

Vowels

1. TIME

Annie has some lovely examples of the Dundee [ɛː] in *I, five
(fev) or six, we used tae cry (creh) them, steak pie (peh) an tatties,
died, the dye (deh) works*. Note, however, that she keeps the SSE
diphthong in the vowels that the Scottish Vowel Length Rule predicts as short: *night, wifie* and *bridie*.

2. WAY

She has a diphthong in *weyst* [wɛist] and *wey* [wɛːi]; note the
[ɪ] in *pastry* and *paper*.

3. CAT

She has a back [ɑ] in *lang, hard, baggie* etc. There is even a
hint of an /ɒ/ before the nasal in *swankier*, a feature which our
Aberdeen speakers demonstrate. Note particularly the [ɑ] in *sawdust, sang, awa, twa*. This is also the vowel which appears before
/l/, even if the /l/ has been lost: *all > aa, aathing* ('allthing' =
everything), *aulder, dollies*.

---

[12] today

4. FULL

/u/ before /l/, where the /l/ is not lost appears as [ʌ] as in *full*.

5. BIT

/ɪ/ varies but is often so close to [ʌ] as to be indistinguishable, so that *mill* and *hill* rhyme with *full* and *dull*. Other examples of this vowel can be heard in *shillin, shift, whistle. Pastry, paper* and *sherry* have a highish [ɪ].

6. BET

/ɛ/ usually has the same value as in SSE but listen for the /ɪ/ in *shirry*.

7. HOOSE

SSE /ʌu/ words like *house* appear as [ʉ] *ben the hoose, flooers, doon* and this falls together with many <oo> words like *took, look*.

8. GUID

Some <oo> words are fronted as in *good* [gɪd], *lifted his hand tae* ye [tɪ]. *Boots* has a pronunciation close to [bets].

9. COT, CAUGHT

Annie regularly raises /ɔ/ sometimes as far as [o]: *mornin, bobbins, clock* etc.

10. BAIT

/e/ occasionally gets raised towards [ɪ] becoming less tense: *place, pastry, paper*. This is a very typical Dundee feature.

11. Note the extra vowel in *perm* [pɛrəm].

Words to listen to

aafie, yaised, mornin, ging, Setterday, twel o'clock, ben the hoose, five or six, whistle, shift, bobbins, baggie, full, box, weyst, wemen, barrae, potty, cry, sawdust, floors, ane, awa doon, hill, shirty, aulder, aathing, braa, ay, hame, pie, tatties, younger, pastry, swankier, whaur, afore, dollies, cried, dye, paper, awaa wi masel, five shillinny perm, boots, gless, tae, died, Broon, Brown, ay, awa, job, dyein, guid, retired, drink.

Jean

Beechwood wisnae far fae Lochee... an there was a big... em... Cox's Mill in Lochee and I could remember at the school, comin hame for yer lunch, for yer denner an... the... queues and queues o people just aa leavin the mills like, goin home for their dinner you know and the... the women wi their heidsquares on tae keep the

stoor[13] off their heid, you know, aff their hair – I remember
that. Cos the... the Lochee High Street would be full o
workers, you know, and ye kent they were workers cos
they were dead busy, you know... hurryin tae get hame
and hurryin h... tae get back tae work. An I remember the
bummer.[14] There was... eh... a bummer at 12 o'clock that
that was them stoppin work, an then the bummer at
1 o'clock that was for them tae start. Then there was
a bummer at five to one as well, right. So ye'd ken that
ye'd five minutes tae get tae yer work.
Well, a big family; I just remember like there was seven
o us which is no really that a great big family, when you
consider like there was fourteen, fifteen that... that lived
up the same close[15] as us. [I] just remember loads o bairns
playin ootside... em... skippin ropes and playin... eh...
Whirly Dab and that was a lassies' game. Well ye threw
the ba up, right, and ye whirled roond and caught it, right?
An then ye did the same... like there was a sequence o
movements that ye made whirlin roond, then when ye got
through the hale sequence, I think there was aboot eight
sequences, that ye had to go through o this, throwin the
ba up and whirlin roond and catchin it. Then ye would go
to Double Whirly Dab, right. So [when] you would go
through it and then whirl twice and catch it. And if ye were
really good ye could go through the hale sequence three
times daein three whirlies, right, [where] it would be under
yer right leg an then it would be under yer left leg and then
it would be backarties that way and then backarties that
way, right. So it was a hale sequence that ye went through,
that was Whirly Dab.

Things to note in Jean's Dundee

Jean uses a lot of SSE forms mixed in with Dundee forms. Note
the vocabulary code-switch between *lunch* and *denner*.

Intonation

She keeps a level pitch until the end of each utterance when she
regularly shows quite a noticeable rise.

---

[13] dust

[14] factory hooter

[15] tenement entry

Mouth Position

Quite far back.

Consonants

Jean has glottal stops as alternatives to /t/ and /t/ is often glot-talised but not nearly to the same extent as our Glasgow and Edinburgh speakers.

Vowels

1. TIME

Jean makes irregular use of the Dundee [ɛ:]. Within the space a few words she has an SSE *five* followed by a Dundee *fehv*.

2. CAT

For /a/, she has a back [ɑ] in *catching, backarties* etc.

3. She has the [ɑ:] sound where 1-vocalisation has occurred as in *aa* and *ba*.

4. FULL

In /u/ words, where /l/ has not been lost, she has [ʌ] as *in full*.

5. HOOSE

Stoor, roond, aboot and *hoose* all have [ʉ(:)], with some, but not much, lip rounding. She includes *good* in this category.

6. Note the [ɛ] in *family* and *game*.

Words to listen to

denner, mills, heidsquares, stoor, high, full, five (both pronunciations), *family, aa, game, ba, catchin, backarties*.

Marilyn

MARILYN: *We played at ropes, boxes*[16] *on the... on the pavement. The pavements had eh... eh... the pavin slabs were sort o offset, so you could... we didna have to draa the lines the way other fowk had to dae on tar. We had the pavin slabs, right, and we just had to draa the numbers. So we'd play at boxes an ropes, skippin. Eh... we'd put a rope bet... between the polies in the backies.*[17] *Then we'd play roonders an aa wi a bat.*

We used to go to the baths a lot cos there was baths in Lochee... still there of coorse... em... ken how they aa have changing rooms now an locks an a the rest o it now.

---

[16] hopscotch

[17] poles for washing lines in the back yards

*Well it was just banks[18] but... when the banks were aa full
ye'd go down tae the dungeons. Oh... it was dead scary
wi aa the pipes an aa(t)hin but it was warm because ye
put yer claes on the pipes an, uh... a the big forkies on yer
claes an aa(t)hing when ye were getting yer claes on again.
What dae ye cry them? What's the real name for forkies?
Forky tailies? They earwigs? Wi [the things on...]*

*Em... sometimes we'd go doon tae the... the baths doon
the toon whar... see whar the Leisure Centre is now
in Dundee. And we had a ladies' pool an a laddies' pool...
Ladies an Laddies! (laugh) and eh... the Mixed Pool. It was
braa. An... in the Ladies' Pool, there was showers afore ye
go in of coorse, the wey there aye is... and there was... em...
footbath, right? It was [a] lang trough just white, like a big,
lang, narrae bath. And... em... we aye wondered whit this
wis... but it wis for washin yer feet afore you go in the bath.
But twa wee lassies could get in it wi yer feet touchin and...
eh... the tap was in the middle so you could get your heel
on the tap tae fill it up wi mair hot water. So naebody ever
got their feet washed there was aye somebody lying in the
footbath. The Lochee baths was right across frae St Mary's,
Lochee, the primary school that we went to, and sometimes
we'd nip into the washie[19] tae get a heat.*

CA: *So do you reckon Dundee's a... a chilly place?*

MARILYN: *Oh it is, yeh... It's freezin especially... but I was
gonnae say especially doon here on the Perth Road... but,
near the water... but the snaa disnae lie here. No like awa
back in the schemes,[20] ken. When it snaas here it it disna
last lang.*

*I like Dundee... because it's near aa place[21] – ken whit I
mean? Its near the hills, it's right in the centre: it's an hour
tae Edinburgh an hour an a half tae Glesca,[22] ken, Dundee
gets forgotten.*

I've had walks about the place, an ye turn some corners

---

[18] benches
[19] public laundry facility (the steamie)
[20] housing development
[21] everywhere
[22] Glasgow

and here's [a] bonny, wee group o hooses that was waste
ground afore... ken whit I mean, it's braa. An fowk are
able to buy a bonny wee hoose an a gairden, instead
o bein stuck up the multis or whatever, ken whit A mean
(Which isnae what fowk want anyway, ken).

   Here's Ben!

CA: *Hello!*

BEN: *Hiya!*

MARILYN: *I'm sure I telt ye tae clean up the kitchen afore*
I went oot.

BEN: *I ken. But I woke up at twelve.*

MARILYN: *I'm no carin. It's aa left for ye, ye're gonna dae it.*
Ay.Ye needna pit yer hand oot if ye dinna.

BEN: *I've got a job.*

MARILYN: *Ay, but it's aa spent. Ye bought a skateboard,*
ye bought (th)e... troosers. Ay, he's no even had a pey
an all the stuff he's had oot o that shop.

Things to note in Marilyn's Dundee

Intonation

Marilyn is an animated speaker who uses a wider pitch range than our other Dundee examples.

Mouth position

Quite far back.

Consonants

1. Although there is complete and partial substitution of /t/ by glottal stops, this is not so regular as in Glasgow and Edinburgh.
2. She has a slight tendency to substitute [h] for /θ/ in *aa(t)hing*.
3. /ð/ is not pronounced in *claes/clothes*.

Vowels

l. TIME

   She frequently uses the Dundee [ɛ:] as in *cry, buy*, but not always: for example, in ... *the wey there aye is* ... you can hear the higher [ɛ:i] diphthong in *wey* just slightly different from the *aye* diphthong which is closer to the General Scots [a:e].

2. WAY

   The [ɛ(:)i] diphthong is used regularly in *wey/way, pey/pay*.

3. CAT

   /a/ is a fairly back [ɑ]. This is the vowel used for the large number of Scots words which are in this group: *lang, warm, walk, washin* etc.

In *banks*, there is some rounding, a feature more typically associated with Aberdeen.

4. OLD

The vowel in *draa* (draw), *braa* (braw) etc and when /l/ is lost in *aa*, *ba(ll)* etc is also a back [ɑ:].

5. Note the [ɛ] in *games, narrae* (narrow).

6. There is an [ʌ] in *found* and *ground*.

7. The final [e] is very easy to hear in *narrae*.

Words to listen to

didna, draa, fowk, polies, backies, twa, games, lang, skite, wonders, ba, baths, banks, warm, aa(t)hin, claes, cry, doon the toon, pool, afore, coorse, wey, narrae, washin, washie, snaa, aa place, hills, hour, walks, corners, hooses, buy, gairden, pey.

Ben

CA: *[What's yer board like?]*

BEN: *[Eh.] There aa different, depends on what ye like: some people like fat boards, some people like skinny [yins]. But it just depends on yer taste in... I dinna ken... whatever ye skate, ramp or street.*

It's just like people probably prefer a wider board for skatin the ramp and then people might want a wee board for skatin the street for flippin it about; but it just depends what ye like.

CA: *So do you do tricks ?*

BEN: *Ay.*

CA: *What sort of things do you do?*

BEN: *Ay... you do all sorts: just jumping up pavements an jumpin aff stairs, o... over walls an that. [Ye] see the rollerbladers daein it on the handrail, ken in the toon: but they're useless... it's all arms an legs flappin about – not good at all...*

CA: *You're not interested in rollerblading?*

BEN: *Nah... I hate them.*

CA: *Why do you hate them?*

BEN: *Cos they get in the wey [...] wax stuff up... Too much wax jist spells oot death. An ye jist faa aff.*

CA: *That just makes ye slip?*

BEN: *Mmm... Ye just land on it... it's just like ice, but cos they've got plastic boots, ken, it's kinna stickier... so that's the only problem. They... they're ayeways like doin stuff that we skate on... an just... they come along... see us skatin [an] wax it up. We go (t)ae skate it an... fa.*

CA: *The shop ye work in sells snowboards?*

BEN: *They're expensive though... phew!*

CA: *Much more expensive than a skateboard?*

BEN: *Oh ay... about four/five times as much... There's mair technology involved... ken in makin the board an all the layers and edges and stuff... it's pure technical. I dinna ken much aboot it yet, but there is a lot more to it than skatin.*

Things to note in Ben's Dundee

Intonation

Ben has the level Dundee intonation with only slight falls or rises at the end of utterances. The flat tone is perhaps exaggerated by the 'non-committal' attitude of youth.

Mouth position

Quite far back.

Consonants

1. He uses a lot of glottal stops.

2. In *-ing* words, he regularly substitutes [in] for [iŋ].

3. The [nd] consonant cluster is often simplified to [n] as in *handrail, kinna*.

Vowels

1. Ben used the Dundee [ɛ:] in *ay, five* but note that the word *ayeways* [aewɪz] is formed from *aye* and not by l-vocalisation of *always*.

2. He has [ɛ:i] in *wey.*

3. He uses an [ɑ] vowel in *want* and *faa*

Words to listen to

    fat, ramp, want, off, handrail, wey, faa, kinna, ayeways, five.

Chris

I was dead lucky when I was at the school daein ma O-levels. My uncle Jim, he had his own painting and decorating business. So ma mum says, 'You've got a job wi yer Uncle

Jim,' and that was it. So I never really done well in my
O-levels because I kent I had a job to go tae. Painter.
Finished my apprenticeship. Still dae it but I hate it.

Things to note in Chris's Dundee

Like Ben, this young speaker has a very flat intonation pattern.
He is very consistent in his use of glottal stops, using them not
only as an alternative to [t] but also for [k] as in *lucky* and *uncle*.

Dens Road Market

CA: *You don't like Dundee?*

A: *Na. I hate Dundee.*

CA: *Dae ye?*

A: *I've went aff it. For some reason I've went aff it.*

CA: *Ye've got a lovely situation... eh... wi the river, ye know.*
I mean today when I was coming...

A: *Docks, [the] docks and aa that carry on.*

B: *But even the docks is worse noo. Know what I mean?*

A: *No... noth... nothing's changed.*

B: *It's aa the pollution that's in it. I mean aa the oil and aa*
the water an that. The Tey's[23] no clean nae mair.

A: *Nuh. Well it used to be, it used to be clean once a time*
but no now.

B: *No now.*

CA: *Would you have been able to swim in the Tay any point?*

A and B: *No. No. Ye're jokin!*

CA: *Even out at Broughty Ferry, would you...*

A: *Oh, the Broughty Ferry beach, the beach is aa right in*
Broughty Ferry, is it, ye know.

B: *[Course if ye]... if you'd swallaed the water you'd soon*
ken aboot it. Ye know what I mean.

A: *Crocodiles and creepy-craalies.*

B: *Jist aa the stuff [that they] throw in the water doon there.*
Ken whit I mean. They'd throw any(t)hin in it.

A: *Throw bottles and everything in it. I mean they fling aa*
their papers and everything. You['d] never know whit can
happen.

B: *Ye just dinna ken...*

A: *The beach is no the same either.*

CA: *The what? The beach?*

---

[23] Tay

B: *The beach. Broughty Ferry beach is the [worst].*

A: *It's gettin worse. They never dae nothing wi it.*

B: *Nuh. No a tidy beach, ken whit I mean.*

A: *It's a mess.*

CA: *It's a shame. It's a shame cos its a great asset havin the...*

B: *Ay.*

A: *Especially in the summer. It's braa in the summer doon (th)ere. Ah...*

B: *[Aabody] goes to it like, but I mean.*

A: *But they aa sit in their cars. They dinna go to the... they dinna go doon to the sand nor no(t)hin.*

B: *Know what I mean [they sit in their cars, man].*

A: *They aa sit in their cars wi the doors open, ken. So... i... in other words they're tryin to say 'I'm no goin doon to that beach. You never know what's in it.'*

B: *That's right.*

Things to note in the Dens Market speakers
Intonation

Even although the speakers are animated, they maintain a level plateau with a final rise.

Mouth position

The back position of /a/ is clearly heard as [ɑ] in CAT words. The /ɔ/ as in *docks, Broughty, go* can also clearly be heard as a more retracted vowel than in Edinburgh and Glasgow.

Consonants

1. The glottal stop is used very frequently as an alternative to /t/.
2. The /l/ in *bottles* is quite close to [o].
3. Initial /ð/ may be lost as in *It's braa in the summer doon (th)ere.*

Vowels

1. WAY

   Speaker B provides a good example with his reference to the river *Tay > Tey* pronounced as [tɛi],
2. There are lots of examples of [ɑ(:)] where [ɔ(:)] would be expected in SSE, Glasgow and Edinburgh: *aa, braa* and even *creepy-craalies.*
3. TIME

   The Dundee [ɛ(:)] appears very clearly in *tryin* but it is not used all the time.

4. Words ending in <-ow> are represented by *swallae* where the final vowel is a definite [e].

Words to listen to

docks, changed, aa the water an that, Tey, nae mair, swallaed, creepy-craalies, bottles, they never dae nothin wi it, tryin.

ABERDEEN

The speech of north east Scotland is very different from that of the central belt. It is often referred to as the 'Doric'. This term was first used by Allan Ramsay in 1721, comparing his use of dialect to that of the Greek poet, Theocritus. In the nineteenth century, it was applied to country speech, particularly that of the Scottish Lowlands. Only later it was adopted by the people of the north east to describe their own dialect. The pride which north-easterners take in their local speech is reflected in the fact that they are less likely to modify their accent for reasons of class or formality than Glasgow or Edinburgh speakers. Older middle class speakers are less likely to see SSE as their first language and will use local dialect to fellow Aberdonians.

Intonation

There is a tendency to keep on a high plateau of pitch, typically with a rise at the end of phrases. Joyce has a slightly exaggerated rise. Ileen is more subtle. Jean and Bill often have final dips. Changes in pitch are stepped rather than gradual.

Many words show a tendency to reduce the contrast between stressed and unstressed syllables *kippers, goldfish, Aberdeen, chemicals*. The taxi driver has some good examples: *affluent, technology, excitin*.

Mouth position

The tongue is retracted. Lip movement is minimal with reduced rounding of HOOSE /ʉ/, BOAT /o/ and CAUGHT /ɔ/ words. Try keeping the top lip spread, covering the upper teeth, with lip corners slightly tense and the jaw close, as if you were facing a stiff breeze off the North Sea. Now, if you try to yawn without opening your mouth and feel the soft palate rise, you can think of the mouth as a cavern. Most of the activity goes on in the space you have just created at the back of this cave. Using this image will help to stop you 'swallowing' the sounds. Imagine the voice focused on the soft palate to achieve the back placing characteristic of Aberdeen.

Consonants

1. The best known feature of Aberdeen speech is the substitution of /f/ for /ʍ/ as in

fit (fat)	*whit*	*what*
faa/faa's	*wha/wha's*	*who/who's*
faar	*whaur*	*where*
fin (fan)	*whan*	*when*
foo	*hoo*	*how, why*
fit wey	*hoo*	*how, why*

hence: *Fit like?* (How are you?) *Foo's yersel* (How are you your-self?) *Faa kens fit tae dee?* (Who knows what to do?) *Faar are ye gaan?* (Where are you going?) These common little words are where this /f/ substitution is most likely to occur but you may hear it in *fite (white), fussle* (whistle) etc.

Our informants, however, are not consistent in their use of this feature. Note also that contact between upper teeth and lower lip is very light. Rather than the upper teeth biting over the lower lip so that they are visible, try contacting the inner lower lip and use only light breath pressure.

2. There is very frequent TH-dropping, especially in *(th)at* also in *(th)ere, (th)eir, (th)e* etc. Look out for pronunciations such as [ahɪŋ] *athing*.

3. There is frequent loss of /l/: *ba(ll), wa(ll)*. Note that this results in an [ɑ:] vowel.

4. In the city, all the consonants tend to be retracted. This is most noticeable with the alveolars, /t/, /d/ and /n/. The dark quality of /l/ is particularly marked in all positions. Of the velar consonants, the back quality of /ŋ/, as in *sing*, can be clearly discerned. The 'smothered yawn' or 'cavern' image will help with /l/ and /ŋ/.

5. The stops have a very firm contact. At the end of words, plosives are often released where there would be no plosion in other dialects. Listen to Joyce: *road, Laurencekirk, esplanade*. There is sometimes final devoicing. Joyce does this in *retired* and to a lesser extent in *esplanade*. Note that in the city of Aberdeen, in contrast with rural areas, the use of the glottal stop is very common. At the beginning of words, before vowels, /p/, /t/ and /k/ are only slightly aspirated. That is to say, they do not have the /h/-quality or breathiness that they have in most accents in this position. The

reduced aspiration is particularly noticeable with /t/ and may even make /t/ sound a little like /d/.

6. /r/ is usually clearly articulated, sometimes even rolled. A uvular pronunciation is not uncommon and is used by the taxi driver, eg *Aberdeen, lumpers, ropes.*

7. Elision, or loss of sounds, often makes words run together:

    going to be > go-ay be [goʔe bi]

and this contributes to the idea that Aberdonians (like other city-dwellers) speak too fast and are hard to understand. It may be necessary to modify the amount of elision for the sake of intelligibility.

Vowels

Vowels which are reduced to the very nondescript central vowel /ə/ in SSE are often longer in this dialect, where stress tends to be levelled out as described above. Our speakers usually raise this vowel towards the height of /i/ but with the middle of the tongue raised. (Try saying [ɑ] in with the tip of the tongue tucked in below the bottom of the lower teeth to get the feel of which part of the tongue is raised. Now say *kipper* keeping the two vowels at the same height but the second vowel slightly further back.)

The generally overriding feature of Aberdeen vowels is their backness. It is essential to get the mouth position well established.

1. MEET, BEAT

The /i/ vowel is made with the tip of the tongue drawn back a little in keeping with the backed position characteristic of Aberdeen. There is rather less lip movement than in SSE because of the slight spreading of the lips even in the Aberdeen neutral or 'starting' position. The list of words containing this vowel is increased in Aberdeen by the addition of

a) many words which have <o> spelling in SSE and <a> spellings in Scots (usually associated with an [e] pronunciation in Scots). So, in Aberdeen, *stone/stane > steen, one/ane > een* and *do/dae > dee.* This last example is used a lot by our informants.

b) some words associated with <oo> spellings in SSE or <ui> spelling in Scots words have an [i] pronunciation, as in *puir* [pi:r]. It is a feature of some parts of the north east that SSE <oo> words, where the vowel is preceded by a velar consonant like /g/, /k/, are pronounced with [wi] as in *gweed* (*good*), *skweel* (school) but for these our informants use forms which correspond with SSE [ʉ].

A small number of SSE /i/ words are pronounced with [ɪ] so that *week, seek, speak* sound the same as *wick, sick, spick*.

2. BAIT

As found in Scots generally, some words which have /a/ in SSE may have [e], such as *mairry, fairm, faintly*. An [e] pronunciation is also found in many words which have /o/ in SSE, such as *hame*. In Aberdeen, a number of these may be further raised to [i] and see *steen* (1a) above. *Way* appears frequently as *wey* [waːe] or [wʌi].

3. BOOT

Our speakers regularly used [ʉ] as in SSE. They do, however raise *to* and *do* to [tiː] and [diː] and see (1b) above.

4. BIT

The /ɪ/ vowel is usually centralised towards schwa [ə] especially in positions of low stress. It is used before /r/ as in *bird* etc, where some lengthening which /r/ produces (see SVLR) makes the vowel very similar to RP's [ɜː] vowel in these words. Of course, RP has lost the /r/. The unstressed pronoun *my* appears as [mɪ]~[mə].

5. BET

This vowel is pronounced with the tongue flat as in Joyce's pronunciation of *Gwen*. The /ɛ/ vowel is sometimes raised towards [ɪ] as in *centre, seven*.

6. CAT

Although the speakers show some variety in this vowel (occasionally you may hear a fairly forward [a]), the vowel in *cat* is usually the best one to demonstrate the back mouth position. The most common pronunciation in Aberdeen is an [ɑ] (Like saying 'ah' for the doctor). This is even more marked when followed by an /r/ (*carries*). Sometimes the reluctance to open the jaw produces a closer, but still unrounded, sound, nearer to [ʌ]. Before a nasal there may be some lip rounding to produce [ɒ], or if accompanied by raising, [ɔ], and there may also be a slight nasal quality in the vowel. Listen to Barbara's *tank* and Joyce's *grannie, Angus*.

7. BOAT

Lip rounding may be reduced.

8. COT, CAUGHT

There is very little lip rounding.

Diphthongs

TIME and HOUSE diphthongs have a very back first part, especially at the end of words. You can hear this in Barbara's *die*, *allowed*.

The pronouns *I* and *my* are *A* and *ma* or *mi* [mɪ].

The negative particle in *canna* and *dinna* is [nɑ].

The vowel in <aw> words *braw, snow* and after loss of /l/ in *a(ll), ba(ll)* is [ɑ:].

The vowel of final *-ly* is [ɪ].

The final vowal in *barrow/barra, window/winda* is [ɑ].

Of is reduced to [ɑ].

ABERDEEN RECORDINGS

Stanley

*My folk were aa travellin folk. So, A was brought up wi
very, very rich culture. In fact, the great folk-singer, Jeannie
Robertson was ma auntie, so A learnt aa the big ballads as
weel so A ken aa the big songs o Scotland. And A also inher-
ited aa this thousands o stories, lore o the travellin folk. But
[I] aye workit in the fish trade, ken, A worked in the fish
trade since A was 15. My first job [A] actually A workit in
the tram cars. We used tae cry it 'the carries'[1] in that day.
And ye only got, ken, jist pittance for pey, just -coppers.
Ye'd tae gie it aa tae yer mither. Ye never had nae claes but
the... the uniform you run about wi day an nicht. An...
(th)en... A went to work in the fish. You got 30 shillings in
the fish. It was hard, hard work but the fish was a fun job
an (th)at. It was a scabbie job but it was a fun job. Ye'd
mair fun wi the folk and A really liked (th)at a lot better
an... A've mair or less just worked in the fish ever since.*
CA: *What did you do?*
STANLEY: *I'm a filleter. So... eh... you get good mon(ey).
But A also used to do a th... Arbroath smokies for
Aberdeen. It was one big firm used to dee it... it was a
Buckie firm did aa the Arbroath smokies and A used to
dee aa the... the smokin o them, the curin of them.
[They] eat them by the thousands.*

Things to note in Stanley's Aberdeen

Intonation

He partially evens out stressed and unstressed syllables: *culture,
coppers* etc.

Vowels

1. CAT
a)   His usual [ɑ] becomes [ɒ] before a nasal as in *auntie.*
b)   Those CAT words which are pronounced with [e] in central
dialect have [ɛ] as in *travelling > trevellin.*

2. He selects Scots forms in many words: *pey, nicht.*

---

[1]   this *-ie* suffix is a feature of Aberdeen word formation.

Words to listen to

> *travelling, culture, auntie, traivellin, fifteen, workit, carries,*
> *pey, coppers, claes, fish, shillings, folk, filleter, dee.*

Ilene

Fish girls were just terrific. A mean, salt o the earth. A mean,
they really are good. A mean, a spade's a spade... eh... if
they've got something to say, it's said, it's dealt with, end
o story. But... eh... A mean, hard-working girls, A mean.
It was cold, cold work and... eh... A mean... they... they'd
their hot dips... phew!... you know, when they're cuttin fish.
An they had their hot pail beside (th)em tae dip in tae their
hands and their hands were like sausages, puddins. [A] still
think there's a lot of women in the fish industry here
although the fish industry has... i... it's on the decline, shall
we say. But... em... no, A would say there's still fishwomen,
ay, fishwives, fishwives.

CA: *You weren't a fishwife yourself, were you?*

ILENE: *No, A didna cut the fish. No, no, no. A used to just...*
A was stock control so... em... It was a different...[...]
we used to go across to the fish-house and pick up aw our
invoices and then we had to go to our own office and...
A remember there was one day, the first time A'd ever seen
a shark. It was a porbeagle shark on a... on a lorry... the back
o a lorry and... eh... the salesman obviously bought it at
(th)e fishmarket and then taken it back to the fish-house
and... eh... A'd treated myself... A was just a young girl...
A'd... eh... treated myself to a new coat, it was like a salmon
pink coat, and some o the fish bree[2] had run off
the lorry on tae ma coat and the smell just would not
come out o that coat. An A... A never liked that coat again.
A mean, A'd washed it, dry clean... [A... we... A] started
off at the dry cleaners. A'd washed it and A never liked
that coat again.
Oh, ay. A was really annoyed because it was... it was a
bonny colour. A liked it, you know?
There were men... male filleters as well. An, A mean,
A remember they used to get... eh... bones doon their nails

---

2   juice, liquid

and... em... used to get poison, ay... mmm... poison off the
bones and they used to have to go to hospital and come
back and get an injection an get the nail... the bone taken
out, if the bone was stuck... get the bone pulled out. What a
mess! A mean, that's just a hazard o the job. A never ever
heard of anybody cutting themselves.
[A mean] A used to take the bus to ma work and... eh...
used to come along Market Street and... eh... there was
a fish premises called Claben. Now ye always knew the
Claben workers because they smelt. A mean, they dyed the
fish. Ay, kippers and yellow fish an things like (th)at. And
the dye! Their hands were bright yellow... em... A mean, you
know what (th)e nicotine stains are? Well these were even
brighter than the nicotine stains. An you always knew. And
you could smell them. The smell o the... this dye an
the fish an also they smoked the fish as well so A suppose
the chemicals that they were usin to smoke the fish in the
smokehoose... You knew, [s]... the minute you sat down
beside somebody, especially goin home. It would stick to
their hair. The smell would stick to their hair and you'd say
(sniff) 'fishworker', right away, you know? But A mean,
they wore wellies and, A mean, Am sure the back o their
legs must hae been marked by the wellies. [A mean] they
must have had rings round their legs wi the wellies but...
eh... no, no, they were [the] salt o the earth, as A say.
It was good fun.

Things to note in Ilene's Aberdeen

Intonation

Ilene's pitch is very even. Slight rises are common at the end of
phrases but these are subtle. She levels out the contrast between
stressed and unstressed syllables: *control, office, filleters.*

Mouth Position

The jaw does not open wide. This gives a very close quality to her
vowels. She has the usual Aberdeen backness.

Consonants

1. She regularly uses the glottal stop as an alternative to /t/.
2. Her stops are firmly articulated as in *terrific, spade,* so that she

seems to linger over them. Note the loss of aspiration in the voiceless stops /p/, /t/, /k/.

3. She has very dark [ɫ]s as in *filleter*.

4. There is a slight palatal quality to her /h/, especially under stress, as in *fish-house*.

Vowels

1. BOAT

The close jaw position raises this vowel as can be heard in *story, cold, coat, bones*.

Diphthongs

TIME

She has a very back first part in this diphthong. You can hear it clearly in *dye*.

Words to listen to

terrific, spade, cold, fish-house, shark, myself, coat, filleters, bones, poison, take, sure, back, salt, earth.

Taxi driver

TAXI DRIVER: *A lived in Aberdeen aw my life, ay... eh... but A do travel around a fair bit.*

CA: *Have you noticed a lot of changes in Aberdeen, you know, since...*

TAXI DRIVER: *Lots of changes. Yes. Especially since (th)e oil came. A lot of the traditional industries have died... eh... Granite's finished. The fishin is practically finished... eh... and although there's still money in Aberdeen, it's... eh... still affluent because of the oil, but A don't know what's going to happen when it goes.*

CA: *Is there a danger that it might go?*

TAXI DRIVER: *Oh, it's definitely levelled out now although they say (th)at (th)ere's still twenty years left... eh... new discoveries and... em... just... eh... new technology.*

CA: *Did you work in oil at all yourself?*

TAXI DRIVER: *Yes. Ay. A went offshore for... eh... ten years. I enjoyed the money. A enjoyed the time off. But the actual job itself, [it] leaves a lot to be desired. But at that time the job was excitin because it was mainly construction. So every time you went oot (th)ere was something new happening. An there was always lots of men on the job. Whereas once*

a platform's in production, it's... eh... much quieter...
eh... although it's more dangerous apparently because
it's live then.
[A wa...] A was a fishmarket porter for a while. That's... eh...
discharging ships. Ay... boats... fishin boats. It was a good
job. (Th)at was the best job in Aberdeen at one time,
ay, either the docks or the fish dock. Which was... eh...
'lumpin' as they caaed it.
CA: *What [does] 'lumpin' [mean]?*
TAXI DRIVER: *(Th)at was just the name that fish porters got.*
It was just... ah... ah lumpers they used to be caaed but...
eh... unfortunately it's gone as well. The National Dock
Labour Board's no longer exist[ed]. The... the dockers are
now sort o free agents and they work directly for a
Stevedorin company and the... the lumpers who were...
eh... under Dock Labour Board as well are the same. A...
A think there's only a handful[s] of guys still go down there.
Eh... mostly crews land their own fish now.
A used to enjoy going to school and coming from school.
A actually enjoyed my time at school as well, funnily
enough. An A remember we used to play oot in the streets
at night, well, after school hours. And... eh... the mothers
used to play out in the street. Used to play ropes. A mean
if your mother couldna... couldna skip, A mean there was
something wrong wi her (laugh).

Things to note in the taxi driver's Aberdeen

Intonation

This speaker has definite rises at the end of phrases. Listen for the rise on *school* both times in *going to school and from school*.

Mouth Position

Typically back. The tip of the tongue is really quite inactive, even in the consonants.

Consonants

The part of the tongue used is always a little further back than it would be for other accents. The alveolar consonants are more in the region of palato-alveolars and the other consonants are similarly retracted.

1. He puts great energy into his stops. You can hear firm, prolonged contact and reduced plosion in *excitin, construction, night*.

2. His /r/ sounds are uvular. You can hear this in *traffic, ropers, lumpers*.

3. He has an [o] quality about the /l/ in *oil*. All his /l/s are very dark: *lot, affluent, levelled*.

Vowels

These are all characterised by the back mouth position. The part of the tongue which is closest to the roof of the mouth is always behind the part which other accents use.

He evens out the stress a little in *excitin, porters, existin*.

1. BIT

The centred quality of this vowel is very noticeable in *fishin, ships* etc. Words which join this group include *twenty* > *twinty, production, Aberdeen* > *Abirdeen, does*.

Diphthongs

1. TIME

In *night* and when he stresses *my*, the first part of the diphthong is very far back.

Elision

Going to happen is reduced to [goʔəhɑpm].

Words to listen to

> *oil, Aberdeen, affluent, twenty, technology, desired, excitin, docks, fish, night, skip.*

Bill

The granite trade now is just nil. There's very little monumental. It was all building type when I was there an (th)en it slowly went doonhill. There was aboot maybe fifty granite yards. Now there's only aboot three. A was [doin out] the ... the big stuff in the granite. Also A was deein ... eh ... the monuments, wheel crosses an bibles, an things like (th)at. (Th)ere was a lot o hand rubbing and ... at (th)at time which is ... which is very, very little now. Ye dinna see that at aa now.

Ian

Granite works. There used to [be]... there was two granite works round beside us: Robertson's and oh A forget the

*other one's names... eh... and A can see the men yet
workin wi their little chisels [em... dr... worked by air].
Drilling out the... the names and they used to get paid
and their wages were in a... a little metal aluminium tin.
An A always remember, whenever any o them got a bit o
splinter... eh... or granite in their eye, their head was tilted
back an a little piece of wood like a pencil wi a little sharp
point was used to nick out the bits of gla... out [o]... the
bits o granite out of their eyes. An (th)en it was half past
four for finishin or five. A think it was five then... there
was no bell went. He just took a hammer and he hammered
on a... a bit o wood an (th)ey know (th)at was... that was
their time up, ye know.*

Things to note in Bill and Ian's Aberdeen

Intonation

Bill has a very even plateau of pitch with some final dips and occasional final rises. By contrast, Ian gives a very clear demonstration of the final rises that we can hear in many Aberdeen speakers.

Words to listen to

*aboot, deein, monuments, dinna see, aluminium, whenever,
back, wood.*

Grace

GRACE: *A was born in June '39 an war was declared
in September '39. So my first six years of life was war.
An A c... A still have the same feelin o fear. It's never left
me, because every time the sirens went ye had to run for
a shelter an these outdoor shelters were usually at the
bottom of the garden. So it was either that or, if ye didna
mak it in time you had to go down to the bottom flat o the
tenement an you had to go under [(th)eir] beds or under
their tables, because the bombing was so bad you couldna
get outside. Em... an A used to be terrified if there was
anyone in an army uniform, because I used to think it
was (th)e Germans. But as they used to say in my day,
the 'Gerries'.*

BILL: *The Gerries*

GRACE: *And A used to think it was the Gerries come to kill me.*

CA: *Oh dear!*

GRACE: *Because that was yer first years o life an if ye hear o wars in ither countries I do tend to think about the little eens[3] because (th)at's how I felt and they must feel the same.*

Our neighbour doonstairs was a... a cook on a fishing boat and when he was at hame we used to sit and wait for him to come oot with wir[4] cakes of whatever he was doin. And I remember he used to come out wi crab... fingers. We used to sit and eat them. And weddins in that days were held in the hoose and ye [did] yer ain caterin so if... if a... whoever had a weddin in that tenement, aa the kids would sit ootside and they would get some of the things that was...

CA: *The goodies*

GRACE: *... ay... some o the goodies. Some o the fine things...*

CA: *The smackerie.[5]*

GRACE: *... the smackerie, the rubbish (laugh).*

CA: *And what... do you remember, what games you played? I mean was it things like skippin and ball games?*

GRACE: *Skippin and... eh... 1-2-3 o-learie.*

CA: *What's... ?*

BILL: *Leevie-oh.*

GRACE: *Ay, [an] leevie-oh. Hide and sik.*

BILL: *Hide and sik, mhmm.*

JEAN: *An that used to be my sister's favourite game. Cos she used to... she used to mak me hide an she never came to sik me. (laugh) I'm the youngest o seven.*

CA: *So quite a big family?*

GRACE: *My mother had quite a big family and she was one of seventeen.*

CA: *Was she?*

GRACE: *She was that. Of course, they didna aa survive. In that days TB killed a lot o them... em... Her mother was actually, she came from Fittie. Aul(d) Fittie. (Th)at's*

---

3   ones

4   our

5   tasty treats

far she come fae. But the house she was born in is knocked
doon now.
A come aff o fishin folk. Now. I was... when I was born,
I was born with a skin over my hair which they call, A think
my mother pronounced it a see[n]yhoo(d).[6] *And that's*
a Fittie expression and it was like a skin over the top o my
hair. And a fisherman offered her five poun(d) which was
a fortune in that days for the skin and underneath A'd a
mass o curls. Whether my mother took him up on the offer
or no, I don't know. She never said. But that was a fisher
thing and maist o them had earrings, because they believed
that was good for their eyesight.
CA: *You wouldn't leave Aberdeen now?*
JEAN: *Oh, no. I've never really wanted to leave. It's just*
hame... I ken faur I am an A ken fit Am deein.

Things to note in Grace's Aberdeen

Intonation

Grace has quite a high plateau. Like Bill, she quite often has a dip
as the end of a phrase. There is quite a big downward step, for
example in *uniform*:

> *... if there was anyone in an army uniform.*

Her intonation patterns, however, do include the final rise more
characteristic of Aberdeen and she provides a typical example in

> *(Th)at's far she come fae.*

Consonants

1. Grace has Aberdeen /f/ in *far* and *faur* (both forms of *where*)
and *fit*.
2. Initial /h/ may have a little friction audible in the palatal area,
especially where there is some stress: *her mother*.
3. Look out for TH-dropping in *(th)e* and *(th)at*.

Vowels

1. CAT
   The backness of these vowels is easily discernible. This
vowel is also used in *watchin*.
2. *Ane* is pronounced *een*.

---

[6] *Concise Scots Dictionary* has 'seelyhood'. A caul or membrane that
may adhere to the head of a baby at birth, supposed to be a charm
against drowning.

3. BIT

She has a typically Aberdeen centralised pronunciation of this vowel. Unstressed *my* has a monophthongal [ɪ]. Also some /ɛ/ words join this class: *never*, *seven*. Other becomes *ither*. She pronounces *seek* to sound the same as *sick* [sɪk].

4. *Do* becomes *dee* [di:].

5. BET

Grace has quite a close mouth position for this vowel. In *Germans* she is closer to the BAIT /e/ vowel. In some other words she moves towards the BIT /ɪ/ vowel. *September* and *shelter* are between [ɛ] and [ɪ].

Words to listen to

September, never, sirens, shelter, mak, flat, my, ither, eens, cook, crab, fingers, hoose, goodies, smackerie, sik, watchin, seventeen, her, fere, Auld Fittie, earrings, wanted, faur, fit, deein.

Barbara

It's a bittie hard actually, wi haen four jobs. But even though [A've] got four jobs, part-time jobs, they dinna work up tae a full-time job even, cos like (th)e creche, they're two and a half hours, the after school club is three and a half hours, an ma cleaning job is one hour and then my under twelves is only ten hours a month. [It's] still nae a forty hour wik. We're nae allowed pets in oor hoose but we've got a snake. Shona had the snake and she used tae get her lad tae gie it white fish. But I couldna get it tae eat. A'm gaun 'Oh no! It's gaun tae die'. So she bought a goldfish, aboot an inch and a half, say, two inches lang. An she took it hame. An she put it in the snake's water bowl. 'S a water snake. And she fed her little fish and she sat for two hours watchin this fish... snake never came oot an she went doon (th)e stairs again. When I came in she says, 'Ma, go on upstairs an see ma fish.' A saw her fish aa right. It was a great bump in (th)e snake.

The snake had eaten the fish. A mean this is just like three months ago. So, they dinna eat very often. She bought anither fish. It wisna there two minutes an the snake had aten it again. But it's nae gettin my... A've a goldfish.

It's a great big goldfish. I had it first then m... I gave it ma
sister. She bought her big tank an was wantin fish. An she
gied me it back wi Peter Loach. He's aboot (th)at long.
And this is like ten years A've had this fish atween[7] me
and my sister. [An it's] still livin. So there's no way the
snake's gettin it. Well, Peter Loach might eat the snake.
It once... Alan come in one day [an into] the kitchen an it
was lyin on the kitchen flair. It had jumped oot the bowl!
So for a while I had to keep [her] covered because
apparently a weather loach when there's... it's gaun (t)ae
be windy an stormy, it starts jumpin aboot an gaun mad.
Supposed to be predictin the weather.

Things to note in Barbara's Aberdeen

Intonation

This speaker has level pattern, but she shows a tendency to hang
on to the last syllable with a rise at the end of phrases. She levels
out the stress in *goldfish* and *upstairs, anither, sister, kitchen*.

Mouth Position

She has very little in the way of lip-rounding except when empha-
sising *two hours*. Her mouth position is quite close and it is the
back of the tongue that is doing all the work.

Consonants

1. She has a lot of TH-dropping.
2. She has frequent glottalisation and often runs words together
this way: *its gaun (t)ae be* [its goʔe bi]

Vowels

She alternates between a monophthong and diphthong for the
personal pronoun *I*.

1. CAT

She usually has a back [ɑ(ː)] here, as in *hard, half, back.*
Following /w/, there is an [ɑ] in *water* and *watching*. There is
rounding of this vowel to [ɒ] before a nasal as in *tank*.

2. BIT

Barbara retracts this vowel as in *fish* etc. You can hear the
retracted version where she gives extra weight to the lower stress
syllable in *anither, kitchen*, etc. She uses this vowel in *weather*.

---

7   between

Words to listen to

full, allowed, gaun tae, goldfish, lang, water, little, watchin,
upstairs, aten, tank, back, kitchen, flair, predictin, weather.

Joyce

*A've got two grannies. There's ma country grannie an ma
city grannie but A ca them Nana. My da's ma, she bide's
across the road, but she's blin noo. She lost her sight a
couple year ago. So we care for her. An then ma ither
grannie, she's fae the Mearns an she's in a wee nursing
home in Laurencekirk.*

*A've got ae[8] brither, Angus. He's the auldest. Then (th)ere's
my sister Anne. She bides doon in Edinburgh... eh... an my
wee sister, Gwen, she bides ower in Saudi Arabia. Her man
works for British Aerospace. So she bides... she's bade
(th)ere for a few year. She's got a little bairn. Her wee
loonie's[9] caed Roy. Eh... my da retired. He retired fae the
fish. He worked in a fish-hoose doon on the esplanade...
eh... an he was 65 in April.*

CA: *So you're... eh... Aberdeen born and bred, is that right?*
JOYCE: *Mmmm... Torry. My mither moved out to the
scheme[10] wi me, it was just newly built, the scheme, in 1969
an I bide[11] on a scheme. It's kent[12] as Buchan but the bittie
that I bide in's Balnagask... eh... an there's a great big
fieldie in front o us, wi a swing park an aathing an it's
right aside the Bey o Nigg... eh... An we'd a right good
childhood really. We used to play aboot on the verandas
an aathin[13] or else go up the Gramps.[14]*

*(Th)ere used to be a fairm up (th)ere... em... [we] used tae
go an get neeps[15] fae the fairmer up (th)ere for Halloween.
An sometimes go pickin berries for him an aa or howkin[16]*

---

[8] one
[9] boy
[10] housing estate
[11] live
[12] known
[13] everything
[14] Grampian mountains
[15] swedes
[16] digging up

tatties in the tattie holidays... eh... we spent nights playin
two man hunt and British Bulldog an skippin an bas.
Stottin[17] *the bas up against a wa singin ba songs.*
This is some skippin songs:

> *Ca,*[18] *ca the ropie,*
> *Yer ma's awa tae the shoppie,*
> *Tae buy a cake o soapie,*
> *Tae wash yer little dockie.*[19]
> *Am awa in the train*
> *An you're nae comin wi me.*
> *A've got a lad o ma ain*
> *An ye canna take him fae me.*
> *He wears a tartan kilt,*
> *He wears it in the fashion,*
> *An every time he cocks his leg*
> *Ye see his dirty washin.*
> *(laugh)*

Things to note in Joyce's Aberdeen

Intonation

Joyce punctuates her speech with some exaggerated rises at the end of utterances. She levels out the stress in *Edinburgh, nineteen-sixty-nine, Buchan, aathin* etc.

Mouth position

She has the typically Aberdeen position.

Consonants

1. There is a lot of TH-dropping *(th)e, (th)at, (th)ere* etc even when singing.
2. Note the loss of /l/ in *ba*.
3. She makes very firm contact for stops.
4. Joyce gives the best demonstration of a forcefully produced initial /h/ producing a palatal sound.

Vowels

l. BIT

Joyce has [ɪ] in *spent*. She has this vowel centred to [ɜ:] before /r/ in *Laurencekirk* but in *her* the vowel varies between [ɜ] and [ɪ].

---

[17] bouncing

[18] drive, turn

[19] bottom, tail end, rump

With a strongly articulated /h/ this gives hint of a palatal glide when she says *lost her sight* [hjɪr]. There is a quite definite palatal glide in *her man.* [hj3:r]

2. CAT

She has a back [a].

The CAT vowel appears instead of /ɔ/ in *ba(ll)*, *wa(ll)*, *Laurencekirk*. Joyce demonstrates very clearly the Aberdeen rounding before a nasal in *Angus*, but *Gramps* and *grannie* have rather less rounding and some raising.

3. BET

The rather close [e] in *Gwen* gives rather a good indication of the jaw position and the flattened tongue.

4. COT

The raising of /ɔ/ to /o/ can be observed in the line-final rhyme *shoppie*, to rhyme with *ropie* and *soapie*. The raising of *dockie*, although it does not produce a rhyme, at least gives assonance with the other vowels in the line-final words.

Words to listen to

grannies, ca, my, blin, her, ither, Mearns, Laurencekirk, ae, brither, Angus, auldest, Gwen, ower, bade, year, bairn, fish, fish-hoose, espanade, mither, Buchan, fieldie, Bey, aathin, Gramps, fairm (th)ere, skippin, ba, wa, shoppie, soapie, dockie, washin.

Key to Phonetic Symbols

Consonants

Voiceless stops

/p/ as in **p**at
/t/ as in **t**ap
/k/ as in **c**at, ki**ck**

Voiced stops

/b/ as in **b**ad
/d/ as in **d**id
/g/ as in **g**i**g**

Nasal stops (also voiced)

/m/ as in **m**u**m**
/n/ as in **n**u**n**
/ŋ/ as in si**ng**, thi**n**k

Voiceless fricatives

/f/ as in **f**at
/θ/ as in **th**igh, **th**eta, brea**th**
/s/ as in **s**ip, hi**ss**, cat**s**
/ʃ/ as in **sh**ip, **st**ation
/x/ as in lo**ch** (SSE)
/ʍ/ as in **wh**y (SSE)
/h/ as in **h**ot

Voiced fricatives

/v/ as in **v**an
/ð/ as in **th**y, **th**at, brea**the**
/z/ as in **z**oo, bu**zz**, dog**s**
/ʒ/ as in rou**g**e, lei**s**ure

Voiceless affricate

/tʃ/ as in **ch**ip, ca**tch**

Voiced affricate

/dʒ/ as in **j**u**dg**e, **G**eorge, coura**g**eous

Approximants (all voiced)

/l/ as in **l**eap
/r/ as in **r**ip
/w/ as in **w**in
/j/ as in **y**es

Additional consonant symbols (full explanations are given in the text)

[ʔ] glottal stop as used by many Scots in bu**t**, wa**t**er etc.
[ɫ] dark /l/ as in du**ll**. Used in all positions by most Scots,
[ɾ] the tap variant of /r/

Key to Phonetic Symbols

Vowels (as described for SSE)

/i/ as in meet, beat

/ɪ/ as in bit

/e/ as in bay, bait   /ə/ as in hammer

/ɛ/ as in bet

/a/ as in cat, psalm

/ʉ/ as in boot

/o/ as in boat

/ɔ/ as in cot, caught

/ʌ/ as in cut

Additional vowel symbols

[ɑ] as in RP father

[ɜ] as in RP bird, word, heard

[ɒ] as in Aberdeen scampi

Diphthongs

/ʌi/ as in time

/ae/ as in tie

/ʌu/ as in house

/ɔe/ as in boy

Diacritics

:   denotes length

~   denotes velarised

-    denotes centralised

Bibliography

Baxter S. (1982) *Parliamo Glasgow*, Paul Harris, Edinburgh.

Brown B., Currie K. and Kenworthy J. (1980) *Questions of Intonation*, Croom Helm, London.

Giegerich H.G. (1992) *English Phonology: an introduction*, Cambridge University Press, Cambridge.

Hughes A. and Trudgill P. (1979) *English Accents and Dialects*, Edward Arnold, London.

Johnston P. (1997) 'Regional Variation' in Jones C, ed. *The Edinburgh History of the Scots Language*, Edinburgh University Press, Edinburgh.

Kay B. (1988) *The Mither Tongue*, Grafton Books, London.

Kynoch D. (1994) *Teach Yourself Doric*, Scottish Cultural Press, Edinburgh.

Leonard T. (1984) *Intimate Voices 1965–1983*, Galloping Dog Press, Newcastle-upon-Tyne.

Low J.T. (1983) 'Mid Twentieth Century Drama in Lowland Scots' in McClure J.D. (ed) *Scotland and the Lowland Tongue: Studies in the language and literature of Lowland Scotland in honour of David D Murison*, Aberdeen University Press, Aberdeen.

Macafee C. (1983) *Glasgow*, Benjamins, Amsterdam.

McArthur T, ed. (1992) *The Oxford Companion to the English Language*, Oxford University Press, Oxford.

McCluskey M. (1990) *Dundonian for Beginners*, Mainstream.

MacMahon M.K.C. (1995) *Basic Phonetics*, Department of English Language, University of Glasgow, Glasgow.

Mather J.Y. and Speitel H.H. (1986) *The Linguistic Atlas of Scotland (vol 3)*, Croom Helm, London.

Millar J. (1993) 'The Grammar of Scottish English' in Milroy J. and Milroy L, eds. *Real English: The Grammar of English Dialects in the British Isles*, Longman, London.

Munro M. (1988) *The Patter, Another Blast*, Canongate, Edinburgh.

Murison D. (1977) *The Guid Scots Tongue*, Mercat Press, Edinburgh.

Reid C. (1991) *List of Plays in Scots, Compiled for the Scots Language Society*, Glasgow City Council Libraries Department, Glasgow.

Robinson M, ed. (1987) *The Concise Scots Dictionary*, Scottish National Dictionary Association, Aberdeen University Press, Aberdeen.

Wells J.C. (1982) *Accents of English*, Cambridge University Press, Cambridge.

Luath Scots Language Learner

L. Colin Wilson

ISBN 978 1906307 43 1 PBK £16.99

ISBN 978 1842820 260 1 DOUBLE CD £16.99

Suitable as an introductory course or for those interested in re-acquainting themselves with the language of childhood and grandparents.

Starting from the most basic vocabulary and constructions, the reader is guided step-by-step through Scots vocabulary and the subtleties of grammar and idiom that distinguish Scots from English. An accompanying audio recording conveys the authentic pronunciation, especially important to readers from outside Scotland.

This is a fun and interesting insight into Scottish culture. By the end of the course participants will be able to read books and poems in Scots, take part in conversation, and enjoy interacting with Scots speakers.

This gies us whit dictionars niver will gie, a taste o the richt idiom o the thing.
JOHN LAW, Scots Language Resource Centre

Other books in Scots or including extensive use thereof:

The Luath Kilmarnock Edition: Poems, Chiefly in the Scottish Dialect
Robert Burns
Illustrated by Bob Dewar, introduction by John Cairney and afterword by Clark McGinn
ISBN 978 1906307 67 7 HBK £15

North End of Eden
Christine De Luca
ISBN 978 1906817 32 9 PBK £8.99

Parallel Worlds
Christine De Luca
ISBN 978 1905222 13 1 PBK £8.99
ISBN 978 1905222 38 4 CD £9.99

But n Ben A-Go-Go
Matthew Fitt
ISBN 978 1905222 04 9 PBK £7.99

Kate o Shanter's Tale and Other Poems
Matthew Fitt
ISBN 978 1842820 28 5 PBK £6.99
ISBN 978 1842820 43 8 CD £9.99

Shale Voices
Alistair Findlay
ISBN 978 1906307 11 0 PBK £10.99

Nort Atlantik Drift
Robert Alan Jamieson
ISBN 978 1906307 13 4 HBK £15

Scots Poems to be Read Aloud
Edited by Stuart McHardy
ISBN 978 0946487 81 3 PBK £5

Speakin o Dundee
Stuart McHardy
ISBN 978 1906817 25 1 PBK £8.99

The Fundamentals of New Caledonia
David Nicol
ISBN 978 0946487 93 6 HBK £16.99

Burning Whins
Liz Niven
ISBN 978 1842820 74 2 PBK £8.99

The Shard Box
Liz Niven
ISBN 978 1906817 62 6 PBK £7.99

Stravaigin
Liz Niven
ISBN 978 1905222 70 4 PBK £7.99

Gangs o Dundee
Gary Robertson
ISBN 978 1906307 02 8 PBK £9.99

Pure Dundee
Gary Robertson
ISBN 978 1906307 15 8 PBK £7.99

Bard fae thi Buildin Site
Mark Thomson
ISBN 978 1906307 14 1 PBK £7.99

Thi 20:09
Mark Thomson
ISBN 978 1906817 75 6 PBK £6.99

Accent o the Mind
Rab Wilson
ISBN 978 1905222 32 2 PBK £8.99
ISBN 978 1905222 86 5 CD £9.99

Chuckies fir the Cairn
Edited by Rab Wilson
ISBN: 978 1906817 05 3 PBK £8.99

Life Sentence
Rab Wilson
ISBN 978 1906307 89 9 PBK £8.99

A Map for the Blind
Rab Wilson
ISBN 978 1906817 82 4 PBK £8.99

The Ruba'iyat of Omar Khayyam in Scots
Rab Wilson
ISBN 978 1842820 46 9 PBK £8.99
ISBN 978 1842820 70 4 CD £9.99

Details of these and other books published by Luath Press can be found at: **www.luath.co.uk**

Luath Press Limited
committed to publishing well written books worth reading

LUATH PRESS takes its name from Robert Burns, whose little collie Luath (*Gael.*, swift or nimble) tripped up Jean Armour at a wedding and gave him the chance to speak to the woman who was to be his wife and the abiding love of his
life. Burns called one of 'The Twa Dogs' Luath after Cuchullin's
hunting dog in Ossian's *Fingal*. Luath Press was established
in 1981 in the heart of Burns country, and is now based
a few steps up the road from Burns' first lodgings on
Edinburgh's Royal Mile.
Luath offers you distinctive writing with a hint of
unexpected pleasures.

Most bookshops in the UK, the US, Canada, Australia,
New Zealand and parts of Europe either carry our
books in stock or can order them for you. To order direct
from us, please send a £sterling cheque, postal order, international money order or your credit card details (number,
address of cardholder and expiry date) to us at the address below.
Please add post and packing as follows: UK – £1.00 per delivery
address; overseas surface mail – £2.50 per delivery address; overseas airmail – £3.50 for the first book to each delivery address, plus £1.00 for each
additional book by airmail to the same address. If your order is a gift, we will happily
enclose your card or message at no extra charge.

Luath Press Limited
543/2 Castlehill
The Royal Mile
Edinburgh EH1 2ND
Scotland
Telephone: 0131 225 4326 (24 hours)
Fax: 0131 225 4324
email: sales@luath.co.uk
Website: www.luath.co.uk